Crocheted
Scoodies

20 gorgeous hooded scarves and cowls to crochet

Magdalena Melzer

Anne Thiemeyer

Contents

4   Introduction

8   Orange
The new black

12   Evergreen
Made in minutes

15   Hot Red
Stitches in curves

18   Blue Velvet
Simply pleasant

22   Peppermint
Snuggle snood

25   Soft & Cosy
XXL crochet

28   Multicolour
Lacy pattern

32   Mix & Match
Always different

36   Rockabilly
Put a bow on it

39   Black & White
Checkerboard

42   Lady in Red
Zigzag pattern

46 Warm Up
With a cord stopper

50 Coral Reef
Patches of colour

54 Grasshopper
Gnome hat

57 Rainbow
Showing its true colours

60 Grey Shadow
Marls and stripes

64 Soft Waves
Flowing movements

67 Wild Berries
Long fringes

70 Ice Age
Hood in a square

74 Mexican Theme
It's got to have tassels

78 How it's done

90 Crochet patterns

Introduction

If you enjoy crocheting hats, snoods or scarves, then this is the book for you; scoodies combine all these features – and our delightful designs are really easy to make.

There are twenty cosy hooded scarves that won't just look fabulous in winter; their chunky yarns mean that they are also a great way to keep your head toasty and warm.

From elegant and chic to sporty and fun, there's loads of variety to choose from. You're sure to find the perfect scoodie to suit your style.

Happy crocheting!

Magdalena Melzer

Anne Thiemeyer

Orange

The new black

Level of difficulty 2

DIMENSIONS

Hood

Width 26cm (10¼in)

Height 33cm (13in)

Shawl collar

Circumference 67cm (26½in)

Height 16cm (6¼in)

MATERIALS

Schachenmayr original Boston (60yd/1¾oz, 55m/50g) in Esprit Marl (Col 280), 5¹⁄₃ oz (150g), and in Red (Col 30) and Pumpkin (Col 26), 1¾ oz (50g) each

Crochet hooks K (7mm) and L (8mm)

TENSION

In main pattern

with hook size K (7mm)

10 sts and 7 rows = 10.5 × 12cm (4 × 4¹⁄₈in)

In hood pattern

with hook size L (8.0 mm)

9.5 sts and 10.5 rows = 10 × 10cm (4 × 4in)

PATTERN

Page 92

Main pattern

Work Chart A in rounds. The arrow indicates the start ch, the numbers the row changes. Work rnds 1 and 2 once, then repeat rnd 3, changing to Chart B to incorporate decreases where indicated. When changing col, work last sl st in rnd in new col.

Colour sequence

Alternate 1 rnd in Red, 1 rnd in Pumpkin.

Instructions

Shawl collar

See Charts A and B.

Using Hook size K (7mm) and starting at the bottom, ch 64 in Red and join in a ring with a sl st. The collar is worked in rounds.

Rnd 1 (Chart A): Join Pumpkin, ch 3 (does not count as a stitch), 1dc (UK tr) in each ch of ring, using Red sl st into 3rd starting ch (63 sts).

Rnd 2 (Chart A): Using Red, ch 3 (does not count as a stitch), work 2dc (UK tr) into first dc (UK tr), *miss 1 dc (UK tr), work 2dc (UK tr) into next dc (UK tr); rep from * to end of rnd, using Pumpkin sl st into 3rd starting ch (32 2dc (UK tr) groups). Rnd 3 (Chart B, decrease): Using Pumpkin, ch 3 (does not count as a stitch), work 2dc (UK tr) between 1st and 2nd sts in first 2dc (UK tr) group, (work 2dc [UK tr] between 1st and 2nd sts in next 2dc [UK tr] group) 6 times, (work 1dc [UK tr] between 1st and 2nd sts in next 2dc [UK tr] group) twice, (work 2dc [UK tr] between 1st and 2nd sts in next 2dc [UK tr] group) 14 times, (work 1dc [UK tr] between 1st and 2nd sts in next 2dc [UK tr] group) twice, (work 2dc [UK tr] between 1st and 2nd sts in next 2dc [UK tr] group) 7 times, using Red sl st into 3rd starting ch (28 2dc [UK tr] groups and 4dc [UK tr]).

Rnd 4 (Chart B): Using Red, ch 3 (does not count as a stitch), work 2dc (UK tr) between 1st and 2nd sts in first 2dc (UK tr) group, (work 2dc [UK tr] between 1st and 2nd sts in next 2dc [UK tr] group) 6 times, work 2dc (UK tr) between next two dc (UK tr), (work 2dc [UK tr] between 1st and 2nd sts in next 2dc [UK tr] group) 14 times, work 2dc (UK tr) between next two dc (UK tr), (work 2dc [UK tr] between 1st and 2nd sts in next 2dc [UK tr] group) 7 times, using Pumpkin sl st into 3rd starting ch (30 2dc [UK tr] groups).

Rnd 5 (As Rnd 3 in Chart A): Using Pumpkin, ch 3 (does not count as a stitch), work 2dc (UK tr) between 1st and 2nd sts in each 2dc (UK tr) group to end of rnd, using Red sl st into 3rd starting ch.

Orange

Rnd 6 (As Rnd 3 in Chart B, decrease): Using Red, ch 3 (does not count as a stitch), work 2dc (UK tr) between 1st and 2nd sts in first 2dc (UK tr) group, (work 2dc [UK tr] between 1st and 2nd sts in next 2dc [UK tr] group) 5 times, (work 1dc [UK tr] between 1st and 2nd sts in next 2dc [UK tr] group) twice, (work 2dc [UK tr] between 1st and 2nd sts in next 2dc [UK tr] group) 14 times, (work 1dc [UK tr] between 1st and 2nd sts in next 2dc [UK tr] group) twice, (work 2dc [UK tr] between 1st and 2nd sts in next 2dc [UK tr] group) 6 times, using Pumpkin sl st into 3rd starting ch (26 2dc [UK tr] groups and 4dc [UK tr]).

Rnd 7 (As Rnd 4 in Chart B): Using Pumpkin, ch 3 (does not count as a stitch), work 2dc (UK tr) between 1st and 2nd sts in first 2dc (UK tr) group, (work 2dc [UK tr] between 1st and 2nd sts in next 2dc [UK tr] group) 5 times, work 2dc (UK tr) between next two dc (UK tr), (work 2dc [UK tr] between 1st and 2nd sts in next 2dc [UK tr] group) 14 times, work 2dc (UK tr) between next two dc (UK tr), (work 2dc [UK tr] between 1st and 2nd sts in next 2dc [UK tr] group) 6 times, using Red sl st into 3rd starting ch (28 2dc [UK tr] groups).

Rnd 8 (As Rnd 3 in Chart A): Using Red, ch 3 (does not count as a stitch), work 2dc (UK tr) between 1st and 2nd sts in each 2dc (UK tr) group to end of rnd, using Pumpkin sl st into 3rd starting ch.

Rnd 9: Using Pumpkin, ch 1 (does not count as a stitch), 4sc (UK dc), sc (UK dc) 2tog over next 2dc (UK tr) (see "How it's done"), *3sc (UK dc), sc (UK dc) 2tog over next 2dc (UK tr); rep from * 8 more times, work 1sc (UK dc) in each dc (UK tr) to end of rnd, sl st into first sc (UK dc) of rnd (46 sts). Fasten off.

Hood

Attach Esprit Marl to stitch 24 of the shawl collar (middle of front). The hood is worked in rows.

Row 1: Using Hook L (8mm), ch 1 (does not count as a stitch), work 1sc (UK dc) into each st of the previous rnd starting with stitch 24, turn (46 sts).

Row 2: Ch 1 (does not count as a stitch), work 1sc (UK dc) into each st, turn.

Repeat Row 2 another 28 times. (hood height approx. 28cm[11in]).

Row 31: Ch 1 (does not count as a stitch), 19sc (UK dc), (sc [UK dc] 2tog) 4 times, 19sc (UK dc), turn (42 sts).

Row 32: Ch 1 (does not count as a stitch), 42sc (UK dc), turn.

Row 33: Ch 1 (does not count as a stitch), 17sc (UK dc), (sc [UK dc] 2tog) 4 times, 17sc (UK dc), turn (38 sts).

Row 34: Ch 1 (does not count as a stitch), 38sc (UK dc), turn.

Row 35: Ch 1 (does not count as a stitch), 11sc (UK dc), (sc [UK dc] 2tog) 8 times, 11sc (UK dc) (30 sts). Fasten off.

Finishing off

Fold hood in half with the right sides together and sew up the top seam of the hood using whipstitch. Include the stitch loops of the opposite layers with each stitch.

Crochet around the edge of the hood as follows:

Rnd 1: Using Hook L (8mm), join Pumpkin to Front middle st, ch 1, 1sc (UK dc) into same st, *ch 1, miss 1 row end, 1sc (UK dc) through back loop of next row end; rep from * to end of rnd, using Red sl st into 1st sc (UK dc).

Rnd 2: Using Red, *1sc (UK dc) in next ch of previous rnd, ch 1; rep from * to end of rnd, sl st into 1st sc (UK dc).

Joining yarn at centre back, work 1 rnd of sc (UK dc) in Red along the bottom edge of the shawl collar, join with sl st to 1st sc (UK dc). Sew in all yarn ends.

Evergreen

Made in minutes

DIMENSIONS

Circumference 80cm (31½in)

Height 43cm (17in)

MATERIALS

Schachenmayr original Aventica (131yd/1¾oz, 120m/50g) in Tropical Green Color (Col 111), 5⅓oz (150g), and Art Deco Color (Col 85), 1¾oz (50g)

Hook size J (6mm)

TENSION

In main pattern

with hook size J (6mm)

10.5 sts and 9.5 rows = 10 × 10cm (4 × 4in)

In cuff pattern

with hook size J (6mm)

11 sts and 7 rows = 10 × 4cm (4 × 1½in)

PATTERN

Page 91

Main pattern

Work Chart in rounds. The numbers indicate the row changes. Work rnd 1 once, then repeat rnds 2 and 3.

Cuff pattern

Work Chart in rounds (rnds a and b). Work rnd a once, with the sc (UK dc) between 2 dc (UK tr) of the previous rnd, then repeat rnd b, through back loop only.

Instructions

See Chart.

Using Hook J (6mm), ch 85 loosely in Tropical Green Color, join in a ring with a sl st.

Rnd 1: Ch 3 (does not count as a stitch), 1dc (UK tr) into each ch in ring, join with sl st to 3rd starting ch (84 sts).

Rnd 2: Ch 2 (does not count as a stitch), work 1dc (UK tr) into the space before the first dc (UK tr) of previous rnd, work 1dc (UK tr) between each pair of dc (UK tr) in the previous rnd, work 1dc (UK tr) after the last dc (UK tr) in previous rnd, join with a sl st to 1st dc (UK tr) of this rnd.

Rnd 3: Ch 3 (does not count as a stitch), work 1dc (UK tr) between each pair of dc (UK tr) in the previous rnd, join with a sl st to 3rd starting ch.

Repeat last 2 rnds 15 times more. (approx. 35cm[13¾in]).

Fasten off Tropical Green Color and join in Art Deco.

Rnd 34 (Chart Rnd a): Ch 1 (does not count as a stitch), work 1sc (UK dc) into the space before the first dc (UK tr) of previous rnd, work 1sc (UK dc) between each pair of dc (UK tr) in the previous rnd, work 1sc (UK dc) after the last dc (UK tr) of the previous rnd, join with a sl st to 1st sc (UK dc) in this rnd.

Rnd 35 (Chart Rnd b): Ch 1 (does not count as a stitch), work 1sc (UK dc) BLO in each sc (UK dc) of previous rnd, join with a sl st to 1st sc (UK dc) of this rnd.

Repeat Rnd 35 another 5 times. Fasten off.

Sew in all yarn ends.

Evergreen

Hot Red

Hot Red

Stitches in curves

Level of difficulty 2

DIMENSIONS
Hood
Width 28cm (11in)
Height 35cm (13³/₄in)
Scarf ends
Length 125cm (49¹/₄in)
Width 16cm (6¹/₄in)

MATERIALS
Schachenmayr original Lizanne
(60yd/3½oz, 55m/100g) in Esprit
Color (Col 80), 24¹/₇oz (700g)
Hook size N/P (10mm)

TENSION
In pattern
with hook size N/P (10mm)
8dc (UK tr) and 4 rows =
10 × 10cm (4 × 4in)

PATTERN
Page 93

Pattern

Work Chart in rows.

Instructions

See Chart.

Start the hood at the back of the head.

Using Hook N/P (10mm), loosely crochet 12 ch.

Continue working in rows, turning at the end of each row.

Row 1: Ch 3 (counts as a stitch), 1dc (UK tr) in 5th ch from hook, 1dc (UK tr) into next 9 ch, 7dc (UK tr) into last ch, turn work through 180 degrees, work 1dc (Uk tr) into each ch on opposite side, turn (29 sts).

Row 2: Ch 3 (counts as a stitch), 11dc (UK tr), (2dc [UK tr] into next st) 5 times, 12dc (UK tr), turn (34 sts).

Row 3: Ch 3 (counts as a stitch), 1dc (UK tr) into same stitch, 11dc (UK tr), (2dc [UK tr] into next st, 1dc [UK tr] into next st) 5 times, 11dc (UK tr), 2dc (UK tr) into last st, turn (41 sts).

Row 4: Ch 3 (counts as a stitch), 1dc (UK tr) into same stitch, 13dc (UK tr), (2dc [UK tr] into next st, 1dc [UK tr] into next 2 sts) 5 times, 11dc (UK tr), 2dc (UK tr) into last st, turn (48 sts).

Row 5: Ch 3, (counts as a stitch), 1dc (UK tr) into same stitch, 14dc (UK tr), (2dc [UK tr] into next st, 1dc [UK tr] into next 3 sts) 5 times, 12dc (UK tr), 2dc (UK tr) into last st, turn (55 sts).

Now work the ch for the scarf onto the two sides. At the end of row 5, work 80 ch. Allow the work to rest for a while, and join new yarn to the other side and again work 80 ch.

Trim the yarn and tighten. Take up the first side of the work again, turn.

Row 6: Ch 3 (counts as a stitch), 1dc (UK tr) into 4th ch from hook 1dc (UK tr) into each ch of the first row of ch, each st across the hood and each ch of the second row of ch, work 1 more dc (UK tr) into the last ch, turn (217 sts).

Row 7: Ch 3 (counts as a stitch), 1dc (UK tr) into same stitch, 1dc (UK tr) in each st to last st, 2dc (UK tr) in last st, turn (219 sts).

Rows 8 to 11: Repeat Row 7 another 4 times (227 sts).

Mark the centre st of the head.

Row 12: Ch 3 (counts as a stitch), 1dc (UK tr) into same stitch, 1dc (UK tr) in each st until there are 14 sts left to work before the centre st, *dc (UK tr) 2tog (see "How it's done"), 1dc (UK tr); rep from * 9 more times, 1dc (UK tr) in each st to last st, 2dc (UK tr) in last st (219 sts). Fasten off.

Sew in all yarn ends.

Blue Velvet

Simply pleasant

Level of difficulty 1

DIMENSIONS

Hood

Width 26cm (10¼in)

Height 23cm (9in)

Loop

Circumference 173cm (68in)

Height 26cm (10¼in)

MATERIALS

Schachenmayr original Boston (60yd/1¾oz, 55m/50g) in Storm Grey Heather (Col 92), 5⅓oz (150g), and in Mint (Col 66), Charcoal Heather (Col 98) and Olive Gold (Col 23), 3½oz (100g) each

Hook size K (7mm)

TENSION

In pattern

with hook size K (7mm)

12.5 sts and 10 rows = 12 × 12cm (4¾ × 4¾in)

PATTERN

Page 95

Pattern

Work Chart in rounds. The numbers indicate the row changes. Work rnds 1 and 2 once, then repeat rnds 3 and 4 (1 stripe). When changing col, work last sl st in rnd in new col.

Colour sequence

Work rnds 1 and 2 in Storm Grey Heather, 1 stripe each (rnds 3 and 4) in Mint, Charcoal Heather and Olive Gold, 2 stripes in Storm Grey Heather, 1 stripe each in Mint, Charcoal Heather, Olive Gold and Storm Grey Heather (total of 20 rnds). When changing col, work last sl st in rnd in new col.

Instructions

See Chart.

Using Hook K (7mm) work 180 ch in Storm Grey Heather and join in a ring with a sl st.

Continue working in the given colour sequence.

Rnd 1: Ch 3 (does not count as a stitch), 2dc (UK tr) in first ch, *miss 1 ch, 2dc (UK tr) in next ch, rep from * to end, join with sl st to 1st dc (UK tr) in this rnd (179 sts).

Rnd 2: Ch 1 (does not count as a stitch), 1sc (UK dc) between first and last dc (UK tr) from previous rnd, ch 1, *1sc (UK dc) between next pair of 2dc (UK tr) from previous rnd, ch 1, rep from * to end of rnd, join with sl st to 1st sc (UK dc) of this rnd.

Rnd 3: Ch 3 (does not count as a stitch), 2dc (UK tr) in 1st ch of previous rnd, miss 1sc (UK dc), 2dc (UK tr) in next ch, *miss next sc (UK dc), 2dc (UK tr) in next ch, rep from * to end, join with sl st to 1st dc (UK tr) in this rnd.

Rnd 4: Ch 1 (does not count as a stitch), 1sc (UK dc) between first and last dc (UK tr) from previous rnd, ch 1, *1sc (UK dc) between next pair of 2dc (UK tr) from previous rnd, ch 1, rep from * to end of rnd, join with sl st to 1st sc (UK dc) of this rnd.

Keeping to col sequence, repeat Rnds 3 and 4 until 18 rnds have been completed in total, ending with Olive Gold.

Place stitch markers on sts 80 and 100 to mark the middle 20 sts (10 ch and 10 sc [UK dc]).

Rnd 19: Using Storm Grey Heather, work as for Rnd 3 to the first marker, dc (UK tr) 2tog over next 2 ch (see "How it's done"), (dc [UK tr] 2tog over last ch just worked and next ch) 8 times, cont in patt as for Rnd 3 to end, join with sl st to 1st dc (UK tr) in this rnd (170 sts).

Blue Velvet

Rnd 20: Work as for Rnd 4 to the first marker, over the dec sts from previous rnd work sc (UK dc) 2tog, (sc [UK dc] 3tog) twice, sc (UK dc) 2tog, cont in patt as for Rnd 4 to end (164 sts). Fasten off.

Finishing off

Sew up the hood using whipstitch. Fold the loop in half with the right sides facing and count seven dc (UK tr) groups on both sides of the decreased dc (UK tr) section. Start the seam at this point and continue to the curve, include the stitch loop of the opposite layer in the sewing.

Crochet around the top and bottom edges of the loop in Charcoal Heather, working 2sc (UK dc) into each unworked ch. Make the sc (UK dc) along the top of the hood tighter so the hood sits a little firmer. Sew in all yarn ends.

Peppermint

Snuggle snood

Level of difficulty 1

DIMENSIONS

Circumference 152cm (60in)

Height 30cm (11¾in)

MATERIALS

Schachenmayr Select Highland Alpaca (45yd/3½oz, 41m/100g) in Mint (Col 2965), 17³/₅ oz (500g), and in Yellow (Col 2918), 3½oz (100g)

Hook size O (12mm)

TENSION

In sc (UK dc) pattern

with hook size O (12mm)

6 sc (UK dc) and 6 rows = 10 × 10cm (4 × 4in)

Instructions

Using Hook O (12mm) and Mint, loosely crochet 80 ch and join in a ring with a sl st.

Rnd 1: Ch 1 (counts as a stitch), sc (UK dc) in 2nd ch from hook, sc (UK dc) into each ch to end, join to 1st ch with a sl st (80 sts).

Rnd 2: Ch 1 (counts as a stitch), sc (UK dc) BLO into each st to end, join to 1st ch with a sl st.

Repeat Rnd 2 another 14 times. Fasten off.

Finishing off

Fold the loop in half with the right sides facing and sew 20cm (7¾in) along the back of the head in Mint.

Top edging Rnd: Join Yellow to any stitch on the top of the scoodie, *4sc (UK dc), 1dc (UK tr) around the post of the sc (UK dc) 3 rows from the top; rep from * to end, sl st into 1st st.

Bottom edging Rnd: Join Yellow to any stitch on the bottom of the scoodie, sc (UK dc) in every st to end, sl st into 1st st.

Sew in all yarn ends.

Peppermint

Soft & Cosy

Soft & Cosy

XXL crochet

Level of difficulty 1

DIMENSIONS

Circumference 65cm (25½in)

Height 46cm (18in)

MATERIALS

Schachenmayr original Lumio Color (82yd 5⅓oz, 75m/150g) in Turquoise-Pink (Col 92), 15⅘oz (450g)

Hook size 0 (12mm)

TENSION

In pattern

with hook size 0 (12mm)

6 dc (UK tr) and 4 rows = 10 x 10cm (4 × 4in)

Instructions

Using Hook 0 (12mm), work 40 ch loosely and join in a ring with a sl st. **Rnd 1:** Ch 3 (counts as a stitch), 1dc (UK tr) in 5th ch from hook, 1dc (UK tr) into each ch, join with 1 loose sl st into the 3rd starting ch (40 sts).

Rnd 2: Ch 1 (does not count as a stitch), (1hdc [UK htr] into the gap after the next st) 8 times 23dc (UK tr), (1hdc [UK htr] into the gap after the next st) 8 times, 1dc (UK tr) into loose sl st from previous rnd, join with a loose sl st to first ch.

Rnds 3-18: Repeat Rnd 2 another 16 times.

Rnd 19: Ch 1 (does not count as a stitch), 40sc (UK dc). Fasten off.

Finishing off

Sew in all the yarn ends. Make a cord 85cm (33½in) long and thread through the front edge, missing alternate rounds. Make 2 pompoms 8cm (3¼in) in diameter (see "How it's done") and attach to the ends of the cord.

Multicolour

Lacy pattern

Level of difficulty 1

DIMENSIONS

Hood

Width 27cm (10¾in)

Height 32cm (12½in)

Scarf ends

Length right 37cm (14½in), left 88cm (34¾in)

Width 14cm (5½in)

MATERIALS

Schachenmayr original Bravo Big Color (131yd/7oz, 120m/200g) in Lime Tweed (Col 371), Fuchsia Tweed (Col 336) and in Candy Print (Col 92), 7oz (200g) each

Hook size N/P (10mm)

TENSION

In Lacy pattern

with hook size N/P (10mm)

11 sts (scarf width) and 6 rows = 15 × 12.5cm (6 × 5in)

In hdc (UK htr)

with hook size N/P (10mm)

6 sts and 5 rows = 9 × 10cm (3½ × 4in)

PATTERN

Page 92

Lacy pattern (scarf)

Work Chart in rows. The numbers on both sides indicate the beginning of the row.

The Chart gives the full width of the scarf. Black symbols = Fuchsia Tweed, grey symbols = Lime Tweed. When changing col, finish the last stitch in the next col.

Instructions

Scarf

See Chart.

Using Hook N/P (10mm), work 12 ch in Fuchsia Tweed.

Row 1: 1sc (UK dc) in 2nd ch from hook, 1sc (UK dc) in each ch to end, turn (11 sts).

Row 2: Ch 1 (does not count as a stitch), 2sc (UK dc), (ch 1, miss 1 st, 1sc [UK dc]) 4 times, 1sc (UK dc), turn.

Row 3: Ch 1 (does not count as a stitch), 1sc (UK dc), (ch 1, miss 1 st, 1sc [UK dc]) 5 times, turn.

Rows 4 to 5: Repeat Rows 2 to 3, changing to Lime Tweed at end of row 5.

Row 6: Ch 1 (does not count as a stitch), 2sc (UK dc), (ch 1, miss 1 st, 1sc [UK dc]) 4 times, 1sc (UK dc), turn.

Row 7: Ch 3 (counts as a stitch), 1dc (UK tr) in next st, (ch1, miss 1 st, 1dc [UK tr]) 4 times, 1dc (UK tr), change to Fuchsia Tweed at end of row, turn.

Rows 8 to 9: Repeat Rows 2 to 3, changing to Lime Tweed at end of Row 9.

Row 10: Ch 1 (does not count as a stitch), 2sc (UK dc), (ch 1, miss 1 st, 1sc [UK dc]) 4 times, 1sc (UK dc), turn.

Row 11: Ch 3 (counts as a stitch), 1dc (UK tr) in next st, (ch1, miss 1 st, 1dc [UK tr]) 4 times, 1dc (UK tr), turn.

Row 12: Ch 1 (does not count as a stitch), 2sc (UK dc), (ch 1, miss 1 st, 1sc [UK dc]) 4 times, 1sc (UK dc), turn.

Multicolour

Repeat Rows 11 to 12 another 32 times, changing to Fuschia Tweed at end of last row.

Now work the last 9 rows from the Chart as follows:

Row 77: Ch 1 (does not count as a stitch), 1sc (UK dc), (ch 1, miss 1 st, 1sc [UK dc]) 5 times, turn.

Row 78: Ch 1 (does not count as a stitch), 2sc (UK dc), (ch 1, miss 1 st, 1sc [UK dc]) 4 times, 1sc (UK dc), change to Lime Tweed at end of row, turn.

Row 79: Ch 3 (counts as a stitch), 1dc (UK tr) in next st, (ch1, miss 1 st, 1dc [UK tr]) 4 times, 1dc (UK tr), turn.

Row 80: Ch 1 (does not count as a stitch), 2sc (UK dc), (ch 1, miss 1 st, 1sc [UK dc]) 4 times, 1sc (UK dc), change to Fuchsia Tweed at end of row, turn.

Row 81: Ch 1 (does not count as a stitch), 1sc (UK dc), (ch 1, miss 1 st, 1sc [UK dc]) 5 times, turn.

Row 82: Ch 1 (does not count as a stitch), 2sc (UK dc), (ch 1, miss 1 st, 1sc [UK dc]) 4 times, 1sc (UK dc), turn.

Rows 83 to 84: Repeat rows 81 to 82.

Row 85: Ch 1 (does not count as a stitch), 11sc (UK dc). Fasten off.

Hood

Lay the scarf out horizontally, with right side facing, and measure approx. 37cm (14½in) from the right edge. Join Candy Print at the edge of an sc (UK dc) row at this point.

Row 1: Using Hook size N/P (10mm), ch 2 (counts as a stitch), working 2hdc (UK htr) into the edge of each lacy row end and 1hdc (UK htr) into the edge of each sc (UK dc) row end, continue until you have 34hdc (UK htr), ending with an hdc (UK htr) into a sc (UK dc) row end.

Row 2: Ch 2 (counts as a stitch), 1hdc (UK htr) into each st to end, turn.

Row 3 (right side): Ch 2 (counts as a stitch), 1hdc (UK htr) BLO into each st to end, turn.

Rows 4 to 15: Repeat Rows 2 to 3 another 6 times.

Row 16: Ch 2 (counts as a stitch), 12hdc (UK htr), (sc [UK dc] 2tog) 4 times (see "How it's done"), 13hdc (UK htr). Fasten off leaving a long length of yarn.

Finishing off

Fold hood in half with the right sides together and, with the long end, sew up the top seam of the hood using whipstitch. Include the stitch loops of the opposite layers with each stitch.

Edging Row 1: Using Hook N/P (10mm) and Lime Tweed, work 1sc (UK dc) into first hdc (UK htr), ch 1, work 1sc (UK dc) into same stitch, work 1 sc (UK dc) into each hdc (UK htr) to the end. Fasten off.

Edging Row 2: Using Hook N/P (10mm) and Fuchsia Tweed, work 1sc (UK dc) into each sc (UK dc) to the end. Fasten off. Sew the ends of the edging rows to the scarf. Sew in all the yarn ends.

Mix & Match

Always different

Level of difficulty 2

DIMENSIONS

Loop in Iris

Circumference 68cm (26¾in)

Height 28cm (11in)

Striped loop

Circumference 64cm (25¼in)

Height 30cm (11¾in)

Striped hood

Width 29cm (11½in)

Height 28cm (11in)

MATERIALS

Schachenmayr original Merino Extrafine 40 (43¾yd/1¾oz, 40m/50g) in Iris (Col 368) and Navy (Col 350), 12⅓oz (350g) each, and in Lime (Col 374), 10⅗oz (300g)

Hook size M/N (9mm)

6 buttons, 3mm (1/10in) diameter

Decorative button, 1cm (½in) diameter

TENSION

In main pattern

with hook size M/N (9mm)

11 dc (UK tr) and 5 rows = 10 × 10cm (4 × 4in)

Main pattern

The loops and hoods are worked in rows or rounds of dc (UK tr). Work only in the back loop of a stitch, as this creates the ribbed effect.

Striped loop (worked in rounds)

(Photo on left)

Using Hook M/N (9mm) and Navy, loosely crochet 64 ch and join in a ring with a sl st.

Rnd 1: Ch 3 (counts as a stitch), 1dc (UK tr) in 5[th th] ch from hook, 1dc (UK tr) into each ch, sl st into the 3rd starting ch (64 sts).

Rnd 2: Turn to work the rnd in the opposite direction, ch 3 (counts as a stitch), 63dc (UK tr) BLO, change to Lime, sl st into the 3rd starting ch.

Rnd 3: Turn to work the rnd in the opposite direction, ch 3 (counts as a stitch), 63dc (UK tr) BLO, sl st into the 3rd starting ch.

Rnd 4: Turn to work the rnd in the opposite direction, ch 3 (counts as a stitch), 63dc (UK tr) BLO, change to Navy, sl st into the 3rd starting ch.

Cont to work 2 rnds in Navy and 2 rnds in Lime, alternating between the two colours, until you have worked 16 rnds.

The loop will measure 30cm (11¾in). Add 2 more rnds if desired. Fasten off.

Finishing off

Sew in all the yarn ends, and attach 1 button to the middle of the back, and to the left and right sides.

Loop in iris (worked in rows)

(Photo on right)

Using Hook M/N (9mm) and Iris, loosely crochet 28 ch.

Row 1: Ch 3 (counts as a stitch), 1dc (UK tr) into 5th ch from hook, 1dc (UK tr) into each ch, turn (28 sts).

Row 2: Ch 3 (counts as a stitch), 27dc (UK tr) BLO, turn.

Repeat Row 2 another 32 times. Add more rows if desired. Fasten off.

Finishing off

Fold the loop in half with the right sides facing and sew together over 20dc (UK tr). Leave the remaining 8dc (UK tr) open for the slit.

Using Hook M/N (9mm) and lime, crochet around the top and bottom edge, working 2sc (UK dc) into each row end, and sl st around the slit.

Sew in all yarn ends. Attach 1 button to the middle of the back, and to the left and right sides.

Hood in navy (worked in rows)

(Photo on page 32)

Using Hook M/N (9mm) and Navy, loosely crochet 58 ch.

Row 1: Ch 3 (counts as a stitch), 1dc (UK tr) into 5th ch from hook, 1dc (UK tr) into each ch, turn (58 sts).

Row 2: Ch 3 (counts as a stitch), 57dc (UK tr) BLO, turn.

Repeat Row 2 another 12 times.

The hood should measure 28cm (11in) after 14 rows, you can add 1 or 2 more rows if you like.

Finishing off

Fold the hood in half and sew, the seam will be on the top of the head. In Iris, make a pompom of 6cm (2½in) diameter (see "How it's done") and attach to the hood.

Using Hook M/N (9mm) and Iris, loosely crochet 1 rnd of crab stitch (rev sc [UK dc]) around the hood. Work 1 st into each row end around the front and 1 st into each dc (UK tr) around the base.

Using Iris, embroider a star onto the side of the hood and attach the decorative button. Sew in all the yarn ends.

Mix & Match

Striped hood (worked in rows)

(Photo on right)

Using Hook M/N (9mm) and Lime, loosely crochet 18 ch.

Row 1: Ch 3 (counts as a stitch), 1dc (UK tr) into 5th ch from hook, 1dc (UK tr) into each ch to last ch, 2dc (UK tr) in last ch, turn work through 180 degrees, 1dc (UK tr) into back of each ch, turn (36 sts).

Row 2: Ch 3 (counts as a stitch), 16dc (UK tr) BLO, (3dc [UK tr] BLO into next st) twice, 17dc (UK tr) BLO, change to Iris at end of row, turn (40 sts).

Row 3: Ch 3 (counts as a stitch), 18dc (UK tr) BLO, (3dc [UK tr] BLO into next st) twice, 19dc (UK tr) BLO, turn (44 sts).

Row 4: Ch 3 (counts as a stitch), 20dc (UK tr) BLO, (3dc [UK tr] BLO into next st) twice, 21dc (UK tr) BLO, change to Lime at end of row, turn (48 sts)

Row 5: Ch 3 (counts as a stitch), 47dc (UK tr) BLO, turn.

Row 6: Ch 3 (counts as a stitch), 47dc (UK tr) BLO, change to Iris at end of row, turn.

Row 7: Ch 3 (counts as a stitch), 47dc (UK tr) BLO, turn.

Row 8: Ch 3 (counts as a stitch), 47dc (UK tr) BLO, change to Lime at end of row, turn.

Row 9: Ch 3 (counts as a stitch), 1dc (UK tr) BLO in same stitch, 46dc (UK tr) BLO, 2dc (UK tr) BLO in last st, turn (50 sts).

Row 10: Ch 3 (counts as a stitch), 49dc (UK tr) BLO, change to Iris at end of row, turn.

Row 11: Ch 3 (counts as a stitch), 1dc (UK tr) BLO in same stitch, 48dc (UK tr) BLO, 2dc (UK tr) BLO in last st, turn (52 sts).

Row 12: Ch 3 (counts as a stitch), 51dc (UK tr) BLO, change to Lime at end of row, turn.

Row 13: Ch 3 (counts as a stitch), 1dc (UK tr) BLO in same stitch, 50dc (UK tr) BLO, 2dc (UK tr) BLO in last st, turn (54 sts).

Row 14: Ch 3 (counts as a stitch), 53dc (UK tr) BLO, change to Iris at end of row, turn.

Row 15: Ch 3 (counts as a stitch), 1dc (UK tr) BLO in same stitch, 52dc (UK tr) BLO, 2dc (UK tr) BLO in last st, turn (56 sts).

The hood will now measure 29cm (11^1/$_2$in) in width.

Add more rows if desired. Fasten off.

Finishing off

Work sc (UK dc) around the front edge in Lime, working 2sc (UK dc) into each row end. Sew in all yarn ends. Make 2 cords, each measuring 20cm (7^3/$_4$in), in Lime, and attach to the sides.

Rockabilly

Put a bow on it

Level of difficulty 2

DIMENSIONS
Circumference 168cm (66in)
Height 20cm (7¾in)

MATERIALS
Schachenmayr original Merino
Extrafine 85 (93yd/1¾oz,
85m/50g) in Black (Col 299),
8⅘oz (250g), and in Cherry (Col
231), 1¾oz (50g)

Hook size I (5.5mm)

TENSION
In mesh pattern with hook size I
(5.5mm)

18dc (UK tr) and 7 rows =
10 × 10cm (4 × 4in)

PATTERN
Page 95

Mesh pattern

Work Chart in rows. The numbers on each side show the rows.

Instructions

Scarf

See Chart.

Using Hook I (5.5mm) and Black, crochet 40 ch.

Row 1: Ch 4 (counts as 1dc (UK tr) and 1ch), 1dc (UK tr) into 5th ch from hook , miss 2 ch, *(1dc [UK tr], 1 ch, 1dc [UK tr]) into the next st, miss 2 ch; rep from * to last ch, 1dc (UK tr) into last ch, turn.

Row 2: Ch 4 (counts as 1dc (UK tr) and 1ch), 1dc (UK tr) into last dc (UK tr) of prev row, miss 2 sts, *(1dc [UK tr], 1 ch, 1dc [UK tr]) into next st, miss 2 sts; rep from * to end, 1dc (UK tr) into 3rd starting ch in previous row, turn.

Repeat Row 2 another 118 times or until work measures approx. 168cm.

Bow

Using Hook I (5.5mm) and Cherry, crochet 10 ch.

Row 1: Ch 1 (does not count as a stitch), 1hdc (UK tr) in 2nd ch from hook, 9hdc (UK htr), turn (10 sts).

Row 2: Ch 1 (does not count as a stitch), 1hdc (Uk tr) in each st to end, turn.

Repeat Row 2 another 13 times.

Make a row of ch approx. 25cm (9¾in) long. Wrap around the bow 3 times and sew into place.

Finishing off

Sew the scarf together to make a loop. For the hood, fold the hood in half with the right sides facing and sew up approx. 20cm (7¾in). Include the stitch loops of the opposite layers with each stitch. Sew the bow onto the scoodie in the desired position. Sew in all yarn ends.

Rockabilly

Black & White

Black & White

Checkerboard

Level of difficulty 3

DIMENSIONS

Circumference 164cm (64½in)

Height 27cm (10¾in)

MATERIALS

Schachenmayr original merino Super Big Mix (87½yd/3½oz, 80m/100g) in White (Col 01), 10⅗oz (300g), Black (Col 99) and Grey (Col 90), 7oz (200g) each

Hook size N/P (10mm)

TENSION

In dc (UK tr) rfp (round front post) pattern

with hook size N/P (10mm)

8 dc (UK tr) rfp and 7 rows = 10 × 10cm (4 × 4in)

Colour sequence

Rnds 1 to 5: In White.

Rnds 6 to 15: In Grey and Black.

Rnds 16 to 20: In White.

Changing colours

When changing colours, work the last part of the last st in the new col to make a smooth colour transition.

In rounds 6 to 15 keep the col that is not being used behind the work, and crochet around the yarn with every second dc (UK tr).

Instructions

Using Hook N/P (10mm) and White, loosely crochet 140 ch, join with a sl st to first ch.

Rnd 1: Ch 3 (counts as a stitch), 1dc (UK tr) into each ch, sl st into the 3rd starting ch (140 sts).

Rnd 2: Ch 3 (counts as a stitch), 9dc (UK tr) rfp, 10dc (UK tr) rbp, *10dc (UK tr) rfp, 10dc (UK tr) rbp, repeat from * to end, sl st into 3rd starting ch.

Rnds 3 to 5: Work as Rnd 2, changing to Grey at the end of Rnd 5.

Rnd 6: In Grey, ch 3 (counts as a stitch), 9dc (UK tr) rbp, in Black 10dc (UK tr) rfp, * in Grey, work 10dc (UK tr) rbp, in Black work 10dc (UK tr) rfp, repeat from * to end, sl st into the 3rd starting ch in Grey.

Rnds 7 to 10: As Rnd 6, changing to Black at the end of Rnd 10.

Rnds 11 to 15: In Black, ch 3 (counts as a stitch), 9dc (UK tr) rfp, in Grey 10dc (UK tr) rbp, *in Black, 10dc (UK tr) rfp, in Grey 10dc (UK tr) rbp, repeat from * to end, sl st into the 3rd starting ch in Black, changing to White at the end of Rnd 15.

Rnds 16 to 20: In White, ch 3 (counts as a stitch), 9dc (UK tr) rbp, 10dc (UK tr) rfp, *10dc (UK tr) rbp, 10dc (UK tr) rfp, repeat from * to end.

Fasten off at end of rnd 20.

Finishing off

To make the hood, fold the loop in half with the right sides facing and sew up over 20 sts. Sew in all yarn ends.

Lady in Red

Zigzag pattern

Level of difficulty 3

DIMENSIONS

Hood

Width 28cm (11in)

Height 25cm (9¾in)

Scarf ends

Length right 35cm (13¾in), left 110cm (43¼in)

Width 22cm (8¾in)

MATERIALS

Schachenmayr original Lova (54½yd/1¾oz, 50m/50g) in Beige-Orange Spot (Col 87) and Beige-Purple Spot (Col 82), 3½oz (100g) each

Schachenmayr original Merino Super Big Mix (87½yd/3½oz, 80m/100g) in Red (Col 31) and Fuchsia (Col 36), 7oz (200g) each

Hook size L (8mm)

TENSION

In zigzag pattern

with hook L (8mm)

10 st (1 repeat) and 6 rows = 10 × 13cm (4 × 5in)

CROCHET PATTERN AND DIAGRAM

Page 91

Zigzag pattern

Work Chart A in rows from right side only. Arrow a indicates the starting ch, the numbers at the right the beg of the row. Work row 1 once, then repeat row 2, joining yarn for each row at the first dc (UK tr) of the prev row, see arrow b, i.e. insert hook in dc (UK tr), draw yarn through, then start with ch 2 as indicated.

Colour sequence

*1 row in Red, 1 row in Beige-Orange Spot, 1 row in Fuchsia, 1 row in Beige-Purple Spot; repeat from * to end.

Instructions

See Chart A for zigzag pattern.

Using Hook L (8mm) and Red, ch 180.

Row 1: Ch 2 (does not count as a stitch), 1dc (UK tr) in 3rd ch from hook, 3dc (UK tr), *3dc (UK tr) in next ch, 3dc (UK tr), dc (UK tr) 3tog, 3dc (UK tr); repeat from * to last 6 ch, 3dc (UK tr) in next ch, 3dc (UK tr), dc (UK tr) 2tog (181 sts). Fasten off. Working in col sequence given.

Row 2: Join new yarn at point b in Chart A, ch 2 (does not count as a stitch), miss 1st dc (UK tr), 4dc (UK tr), *3dc (UK tr) in next st, 3dc (UK tr), dc (UK tr) 3tog, 3dc (UK tr); repeat from * to last 6 sts, 3dc (UK tr) in next st, 3dc (UK tr), dc (UK tr) 2tog. Fasten off.

Repeat Row 2 another 7 times working in col sequence given, ending with Row 9 in Red.

Lady in Red

Hood

With right side of scarf facing, starting at the 4th point and ending at the 9th point of the prev row as shown in the schematic, follow Chart B and continue the col sequence.

Row 10: Join yarn at point a of Chart B, ch 3 (counts as a stitch), 1dc (UK tr) in same st, (3dc [UK tr], dc [UK tr] 3tog, 3dc [UK tr], 3dc [UK tr] in next st) 4 times, 3dc (UK tr), dc (UK tr) 3tog, 3dc (UK tr), 2dc (UK tr) in last st (51 sts). Fasten off.

Row 11: Work as Row 10, joining the yarn at point b in Chart B.

Row 12: This row will straighten the hood. Join yarn at arrow b in prev row ch1, 1sc (UK dc) in same st, (1sc [UK dc], 2hdc [UK htr], 3dc [UK tr], 2hdc [UK htr], 2sc [UK dc]) twice (to arrow c), over the middle dip (not shown) work (sc [UK dc] 2tog twice, 1sc (UK dc) in the middle st, (sc [UK dc] 2tog) twice, 1sc (UK dc), (1sc [UK dc], 2hdc [UK htr], 3dc [UK tr], 2hdc [UK htr], 2sc [UK dc]) twice (arrows c to d), turn (47 sts).

Row 13 (wrong side): Ch 1, 1sc (UK dc) into the last st of the prev row, 17sc (UK dc), (sc [UK dc] 2tog) twice, sc (UK dc) 3tog, (sc [UK dc] 2tog) twice, 18 sc (UK dc) (41 sts).

Fasten off. Cut the yarn, leaving it fairly long.

Finishing off

Use this yarn to sew up the back hood seam in whipstitch. Fold the hood in half with the right sides facing, including the stitch loops of the opposite layers when sewing.

Work 1 row of sc (UK dc) along the long sides of the scarf in Red (see grey area in Chart A), joining the yarn on the wrong side (see arrow c) and working 3sc (UK dc) in each point and sc (UK dc) 3tog in each dip, finish with sc (UK dc) 2tog in last 2 sts. Sew in all yarn ends.

Warm Up

With a cord stopper

Level of difficulty 2

DIMENSIONS

Hood

Width 25cm (9¾in)

Height 27cm (10¾in)

Shawl collar

Circumference 67cm (26½in)

Height 12.5cm (5in)

MATERIALS

Schachenmayr original Merino Extrafine 40 (43¾/1¾oz, 40m/50g) in Pine (Col 377) and Eggplant (Col 349), 5⅓oz (150g) each, and in Chartreuse (Col 374), 1¾oz (50g)

Hook size L (8mm)

Stitch marker

TENSION

In hood pattern

with hook size L (8mm)

9.5 sts and 8.5 rows = 10 × 10cm (4 × 4in)

In scarf pattern

with hook size L (8mm)

5 sts and 5 rows = 6 × 6cm (2½ × 2½in)

PATTERN

Page 92

Hood pattern

Work Chart A in rows. The numbers at the sides indicate the beginning of the row. The letters indicate the col: A = Pine (main col), B = Chartreuse and C = Eggplant. Work each dc (UK tr) rfp stitch (see "How it's done") around the front post of the dc (UK tr) 2 rows below (called dc [UK tr] rfp 2 below in the instructions) Work rows 1 and 2 once, then repeat rows 3 to 8. When changing colours, work the last part of the last st in the new col to make a smooth colour transition.

Scarf pattern

Work Chart B in offset hdc (UK htr) in rounds. The numbers indicate the row changes. Work rnd 1, then continue repeating rnds 2 and 3.

Instructions

Hood

Start at the front edge.

Using Hook L (8mm) and Pine, ch 52.

Row 1: Ch 3 (counts as a stitch), dc (UK tr) into 4th ch from hook, dc (UK tr) into each ch, turn (53 sts).

Row 2: Ch 1 (does not count as a stitch), sc (UK dc) in each st, change to Chartreuse at the end of the row, turn.

Row 3: Ch 1 (does not count as a stitch), *3sc (UK dc), dc (UK tr) rfp 2 below, rep from * to last st, sc (UK dc) in last st. Fasten off Chartreuse.

Row 4: With right side facing, sl st with Pine into 1st st in Row 3, ch 3 (counts as a stitch), dc (UK tr) into each st to end, turn.

Row 5: Ch 1 (does not count as a stitch), sc (UK dc) in each st, change to Eggplant at the end of the row, turn.

Row 6: Ch 1 (does not count as a stitch), 2sc (UK dc), *3sc (UK dc), dc (UK tr) rfp 2 below, rep from * to last 3 sts, 3sc (UK dc). Fasten off Eggplant.

Row 7: Repeat Row 4.

Row 8: Ch 1 (does not count as a stitch), sc (UK dc) in each st, change to Chartreuse at the end of the row, turn.

Repeat Rows 3 to 8 once, then Row 3 once.

Start the dec for the hood curve in Row 16. Mark the middle st.

Row 16: Work as Row 4 until there are 4 sts left before marked st, (dc [UK tr] 2tog) twice (see "How it's done"), dc (UK tr) in marked st, (dc [UK tr] 2tog) twice, dc (UK tr) to end, turn (49 sts).

Row 17: Work as Row 5 until there are 4 sts left before marked st, (sc [UK dc] 2tog) twice (see "How it's done"), sc (UK dc) in marked st, (sc [UK dc] 2tog) twice, sc (UK dc) to end, change to Eggplant at the end of the row, turn (45 sts).

Row 18: Work as Row 6, after the fifth dc (UK tr) ftp 2 below, work 1sc (UK tr), sc (UK tr) 2tog (mark this st as the new centre st), 1sc (UK tr), *1dc (UK tr) ftp 2 below, 3 sc (UK dc); repeat from * to end (44 sts). Fasten off Eggplant.

Row 19: Work as Row 16 (40 sts).

Row 20: Work as row 17 (36 sts).

Fold the hood in half with the right sides facing. Sew up the back hood seam in whipstich, including the stitch loops of the opposite layers. Turn the hood right side out.

Shawl collar

Foundation Rnd: Using Hook L (8mm) and Eggplant, start at the middle of the back of the hood with right side facing, and sl st 21 along the right side of the hood, ch 14 for the middle front, then from the front edge of the left side of the hood work another 21 sl st to the middle of the back of the hood. Finish the rnd with a sl st into the 1st st (56 sts).

Rnd 1: Ch 2 (counts as a stitch), hdc (UK htr) into each sl st BLO and each ch around, join with a sl st into the 2nd starting ch.

Rnd 2: Ch 2 (does not count as a stitch), hdc (UK htr) into space before 1st hdc (UK htr) in previous rnd, *hdc (UK htr) into space before next hdc (UK htr) in previous rnd; repeat from * to end, hdc (UK htr) after last hdc (UK htr) of previous rnd, join with a sl st into 1st hdc (Uk htr) of this rnd.

Rnd 3: Ch 2 (counts as a stitch), hdc (UK htr) into space after 1st hdc (UK htr) in previous rnd, *hdc (UK htr) after each hdc ((UK htr) in previous rnd, join with a sl st into 2nd starting ch.

Rnds 4 to 9: Repeat Rnds 2 to 3 three times, turn after the end of Rnd 9.

Rnd 10 (wrong side): Ch 1 (does not count as a st), sc (UK dc) in each st to end. Fasten off.

Crochet in sc (UK dc) around the front of the hood in Pine and the middle part of the shawl collar in Eggplant.

Cord stopper

Using Hook L (8mm) and Pine, ch 10, join in a ring with a sl st.

Rnd 1: Ch 1 (does not count as a stitch), sc (UK dc) into each ch, join with a sl st to 1st st (10 sts).

Rnd 2: Ch 1 (does not count as a stitch), sc (UK dc) into each st, join with a sl st to 1st st.

Rnd 3 : Work as Rnd 2.

After rnd 3 cut the yarn, leaving a reasonable length, and backstitch a vertical line up the middle to create a tube down both sides.

Cord

Using Hook L (8mm) and 1 strand each of Eggplant and Pine, ch approx 110. Use a safety pin to thread this chain through the second rnd of the shawl collar. Start to the left of the 2 middle front sts and thread cord from front to back, miss 2 sts, thread the cord from back to front. Continue around in this way finishing just before the two middle sts. Use a hook to thread the ends of the cord through the tubes of the cord stopper. Cut off the ends to the desired length. Tie each end securely and trim neatly.

Coral Reef

Patches of colour

Level of difficulty 2

DIMENSIONS

Hood

Width 27cm (10¾in)

Height 31cm (12¼in)

Shawl collar

Circumference 68cm (26¾in)

Height 16cm (6¼in)

MATERIALS

Schachenmayr original Boston (60yd/1¾oz, 55m/50g) in Storm Grey Heather (Col 92), 7oz (200g), in Charcoal Heather (Col 98), 3½oz (100g), and Coral (Col 133), 1¾oz (50g)

Hook size J (6mm)

TENSION

In collar pattern

with hook size J (6mm)

10.5 sts and 10 rows = 10 × 13cm (4 × 5in)

In bobble pattern

with hook size J (6mm)

11 sts and 7.5 rows = 10 × 10cm (4 × 4in)

PATTERN

Page 95

Collar pattern

Work Chart A in rounds. The numbers indicate the row changes. When changing colours, work the last part of the last st in the new col to make a smooth colour transition.

Bobble pattern

Work Chart B in rows. The numbers at the sides indicate the beginning of the row. Work row 1 once, then continue working rows 2 and 3. The sc (UK dc) of the last row of the Shawl collar are shown below row 1.

Instructions

Shawl collar

See Chart A.

Using Hook J (6mm) and Charcoal Heather ch 72, join in a ring with a sl st.

Rnd 1: Ch 3 (counts as a stitch), dc (UK tr) into 5th ch from hook, dc (UK tr) into each ch to end, join with sl st to 3rd starting ch (72 sts).

Rnd 2: Ch 2 (counts as a stitch), 2dc (UK tr) rfp (see "How it's done"), *4hdc (UK htr), 2dc (UK tr) rfp; repeat from * to last 3 sts, 3hdc (UK htr), join with sl st to 2nd starting ch.

Rnd 3: Ch 2 (counts as a stitch), *2dc (UK tr) rfp, 1hdc (UK htr), hdc (UK htr) 2tog, 1hdc (UK htr), 2dc (UK tr) rfp, 4hdc (UK htr); repeat from * to last 11 sts, 2dc (UK tr) rfp, 1hdc (UK htr), hdc (UK htr) 2tog, 1hdc (UK htr), 2dc (UK tr) rfp, 3hdc (UK htr), join with sl st to 2nd starting ch (66 sts).

Rnd 4: Ch 2 (counts as a stitch), *2dc (UK tr) rfp, 3hdc (UK htr), 2dc (UK tr) rfp, 4hdc (UK htr); repeat from * to last 11 sts, (2dc (UK tr) rfp, 3hdc [UK htr]) twice, join with sl st to 2nd starting ch.

Rnd 5: Ch 2 (counts as a stitch), *2dc (UK tr) rfp, 3hdc (UK htr), 2dc (UK tr) rfp, 1hdc (UK htr), hdc (UK htr) 2tog, 1hdc (UK htr); repeat from * to last 10 sts, 2dc (UK tr) rfp, 3hdc (UK htr), 2dc (UK tr) rfp, 1hdc (UK htr), hdc (UK htr) 2tog, join with sl st to 2nd starting ch (60 sts).

Rnd 6: Ch 2 (counts as a stitch), 2dc (UK tr) rfp, *3hdc (UK htr), 2dc (UK tr) rfp; repeat from * to last 2 sts, 2hdc (UK htr), join with sl st to 2nd starting ch, changing to Coral at end of rnd.

Rnd 7: Ch 2 (counts as a stitch), 2dc (UK tr) rfp, *3hdc (UK htr), 2dc (UK tr) rfp; repeat from * to last 2 sts, 2hdc (UK htr), join with sl st to 2nd starting ch.

Coral Reef

Rnds 8 to 10: Work as Rnd 7.

Rnd 11: Ch 1 (does not count as a stitch), sc (UK dc) in each st to end, join with sl st to 1st st.

Rnd 12: Work as Rnd 11.

Hood

Using Storm Grey Heather, crochet the hood onto the shawl collar in bobble pattern. The rnd change for the shawl collar will be at the middle of the back of the hood.

Count to the 27th st from the middle of the back to the left. Join before this st with wrong side facing (see arrow in Chart B).

Row 1 (wrong side): Using Hook] (6mm), ch 1 (does not count as a stitch), sc (UK dc) in next st, (ch 1, miss 1 st, sc [UK dc] in next st) 13 times, (ch 1, sc [UK dc] in next st) twice, (ch 1, miss 1 st, sc [UK dc] in next st) 13 times, leave last 5 sts of previous rnd unworked, turn (57 sts).

Row 2: Ch 3 (counts as a stitch), cluster into 1st ch space, *ch 1, miss 1 st, cluster in next ch space; repeat from * to last st, dc (UK tr) in last st, turn.

Row 3: Ch 1 (does not count as a stitch), sc (UK dc) in last st of previous rnd, *ch 1, miss 1 st, sc (UK dc) in ch space; repeat from * to last 2 sts, ch 1, miss 1 st, sc (UK dc) in 3rd starting ch, turn.

Rows 4 to 22: Repeat Rows 2 and 3 a further 9 times, then Row 2 once.

Row 23: Ch 1 (does not count as a stitch), sc (UK dc) in last st of previous rnd, (ch 1, miss 1 st, sc [UK dc] in next ch space) 10 times, (sc [UK dc] into next ch space) 8 times; (ch 1, miss 1 st, sc [UK dc] in next ch space) 10 times, turn, change to Coral at end of row (49 sts).

Row 24: Ch 1 (does not count as stitch), sc (UK dc) in each ch and sc (UK dc) of previous rnd.

Cut the yarn, leaving it fairly long.

Finishing off

Fold hood in half with the right sides together and, with the long end, sew up the top seam of the hood using whipstitch. Include the stitch loops of the opposite layers with each stitch.

Crochet around the front edge of the hood in Strom Grey Heather. Attach yarn to the st in Coral just left of the 5 unworked middle sts.

Row 1: Using Hook J (6mm), ch 2 (does not count as a stitch), 1dc (UK tr) in same place, work (ch 1, 1dc [UK tr]) evenly 22 times to just before centre of hood, ch 1, 1dc (UK tr) in Coral stripe, work (ch 1, 1dc [UK tr]) evenly 22 times to edge of hood (45 dc [UK tr]).

Cord

Using Hook J (6mm) and Coral, ch 120 turn and work 1 sl st into each ch, starting in the 2nd ch from the hook. Fasten off.

Thread the cord in and out of the dc (UK tr) around the front of the hood. Make a pompom of 5.5cm (2¼in) diameter using all three yarns (see "How it's done") and sew to the tip of the hood. Sew in all yarn ends.

Grasshopper

Gnome hat

Level of difficulty 1

DIMENSIONS

Hood

Width 53cm (20¾in)

Height 30cm (11¾in)

Scarf ends

Length 98cm (38½in)

Width 20cm (7¾in)

MATERIALS

Schachenmayr select Savanti (32⅘yd/1½oz, 30m/50g) in Tundra (Col 4869), 23oz (650g), and Moor (Col 4769), 3½oz (100g)

Hook size N/P (10mm)

TENSION

In pattern

with hook size N/P (10mm)

8 hdc (htr) and 6 rows = 10 × 10cm (4 × 4in)

Instructions

Gnome hat

Using Hook N/P (10mm) and Tundra, ch 17. Row 1 (right side): Ch 2 (counts as a stitch), 1hdc (UK htr) in 3rd ch from hook,1hdc (UK htr) in each ch to the last ch, 2dc (UK tr) into the last ch, turn (19 sts).

Row 2 (wrong side): Ch 3 (counts as a stitch),1dc (UK tr) into the same st, 18hdc (UK htr), turn (20 sts).

Row 3: Ch 2 (counts as a stitch), hdc (UK htr) in each st to the last st, 2dc (UK tr) in last st, turn (21 sts).

Row 4: Ch 3 (counts as a stitch), 1dc (UK tr) into the same st, hdc (UK htr) in each st to end, turn (22 sts).

Rows 5 to 18: Repeat Rows 3 to 4 another 7 times (36 sts).

Row 19: Ch 2 (counts as a stitch), hdc (UK htr) in each st to the last 2 sts, dc (UK tr) 2tog, turn (35 sts).

Row 20: Ch 3 (counts as a stitch), dc (UK tr) 2tog, hdc (UK htr) in each st to end, turn (34 sts).

Rows 21 to 35: Repeat Rows 19 to 20 a further 7 times, then Row 19 once (19 sts).

Do not cut the yarn. Fold the hood in half and sew along the sloping side.

Scarf (work 2)

Using Hook N/P (10mm) and Tundra, with right side facing, work 14hdc (UK htr) into the first 14 sts of the gnome hat on one side, turn.

Row 1: Ch 2 (counts as a stitch), hdc (UK htr) in each st to end, turn.

Repeat Row 1 until the scarf measures 96cm (37¾in) in length. Work the second scarf section in the same way on the other side of the hat.

Finishing off

Crochet 2 rows of hdc (UK htr) around the front of the hat in Moor, working 1hdc (UK htr) into each st. Make a pompom of approx. 10cm (4in) diameter in Moor (see "How it's done") and sew onto the hood. Sew in all yarn ends.

Grasshopper

Rainbow

Rainbow

Showing its true colours

Level of difficulty 1

DIMENSIONS

Circumference 178cm (70in)

Height 26cm (10¼in)

MATERIALS

Schachenmayr original Merino Super Big Mix (87½yd/3½oz, 80m/100g) in Geranium (Col 37), Fuchsia (Col 36), Cyclamen (Col 38), Royal (Col 51), Turquoise (Col 69), Jade (Col 70), Apple Green (Col 71), Anise (Col 22), Red (Col 31) and Cherry (Col 30), 3½oz (100g) each

Hook size N/P (10mm)

TENSION

In Basic pattern

with hook size N/P (10mm)

7 offset hdc (UK htr) and 8 rows = 10 × 10cm (4 × 4in)

Basic pattern

The scoodie is worked in rounds of offset hdc UK htr). Do not insert the hook into the stitch, but in the space before the next hdc (UK htr) in the rnd below.

Colour sequence

2 rnds in Geranium, 2 rnds in Fuchsia, 2 rnds in Cyclamen, 2 rnds in Royal, 2 rnds in Turquoise, 2 rnds in Jade, 2 rnds in Apple Green, 2 rnds in Anise, 2 rnds in Red, 2 rnds in Cherry. When changing colours, work the last part of the last st in the new col to make a smooth colour transition.

Instructions

Using Hook N/P (10mm) and Geranium, ch 130 loosely, join in a ring with a sl st.

Work in the colour sequence.

Rnd 1: Ch 2 (counts as a stitch), hdc (UK htr) into 3rd ch from hook, hdc (UK htr) in each st to the end, sl st into 2nd starting ch (130 sts).

Rnd 2: Ch 1 (counts as a stitch), hdc (UK htr) into the space before the first hdc (UK htr), *hdc (UK htr) into the space before the next hdc (UK htr); repeat from * to end, sl st into 1st starting ch.

Rnds 3 to 18: Repeat Rnd 2 changing col as indicated.

Now start the shaping for the head.

Rnd 19: Ch 1 (counts as a stitch), hdc (UK htr) into the space before the first hdc (UK htr), (hdc [UK htr] into the space before the next hdc [UK htr]) 61 times, (hdc [UK htr] 2tog in spaces before next 2 sts) twice, *hdc (UK htr) into the space before the next hdc (UK htr); repeat from * to end, sl st into 1st starting ch (128 sts).

Rnd 20: Ch 1 (counts as a stitch), hdc (UK htr) into the space before the first hdc (UK htr), (hdc [UK htr] into the space before the next hdc [UK htr]) 61 times, hdc (UK htr) 3tog in spaces before next 3 sts, *hdc (UK htr) into the space before the next hdc (UK htr); repeat from * to end, sl st into first starting ch (126 sts). Fasten off.

Finishing off

Fold the loop in half with the right sides facing, make sure the back of the head is shaped neatly. Sew along 15hdc (UK htr). Include the stitch loops of the opposite layers with each stitch. Sew in all yarn ends.

Grey Shadow

Marls and stripes

PATTERN
Page 92

Level of difficulty 2

DIMENSIONS

Hood

Width 25cm (9¾in)

Height 32cm (12½in)

Loop

Circumference 127cm (50in)

Height 16.5cm (6½in)

MATERIALS

Schachenmayr original Boston (60yd/1¾oz, 55m/50g) in Midnight Marl (Col 282), 7oz (200g), in Charcoal Heather (Col 98), 5⅓oz (150g), and in Storm Grey Heather (Col 92), 1¾oz (50g)

Crochet hooks K (7mm) and L (8mm)

TENSION

In the rib pattern

with hook size L (8mm)

9.5 sts and 8 rows = 10 × 10cm (4 × 4in)

In scarf pattern

with hook size L (8mm)

11 sts and 12 rows = 10 × 10cm (4 × 4in)

PATTERN

Page 92

Rib pattern

Work Chart A in rows. The numbers at the sides indicate the beginning of the row. Work row 1 once, then repeat rows 2 and 3.

Scarf pattern

Work Chart B in rnds in the col sequence. The arrow indicates the start ch, the numbers the row changes. Work rnd 1 once, then repeat rnds 2 and 3 to end. When changing colours, work the sl st to finish the round in the next col.

Scarf colour sequence

*2 rnds in Charcoal Heather, 2 rnds in Storm Grey Heather, 2 rnds in Charcoal Heather, 2 rnds in Midnight Marl; rep from * once, finish with 2 rnds in Charcoal Heather.

Instructions

Hood

Using Hook L (8mm), starting at the bottom edge, ch 23 in Midnight Marl.

Row 1: Ch 1 (does not count as a stitch), sc (UK dc) in 2nd ch from hook, sc (UK dc) in each ch to end, turn (23 sts).

Row 2: Ch 2 (counts as a stitch), hdc (UK htr) in each st to end, turn.

Row 3: Ch 1 (does not count as a stitch), sc (UK dc) BLO in each st to end, turn.

Repeat Rows 2 and 3 until work measures 64cm (25¼in) in length.

Fold the hood in half with the right sides facing and the short sides together. Sew up the rear hood seam in whipstitch, and turn the hood right side out.

Grey Shadow

Loop

Using Hook L (8mm) and Charcoal Heather, with right side facing, starting at the middle of the back of the hood work 1 sl st into each into each sc (UK dc) over the right half of the hood (23 sl st), ch 94, and work another 23 sl st over the left side of the hood from the front edge to the middle of the back, sl st to 1st st to join (140 sts).

Working in the col sequence indicated:

Rnd 1: Ch 1 (does not count as a stitch), *1sc (UK dc), ch 1, miss 1 ch; repeat from * to end, join with a sl st to 1st st.

Rnd 2: Ch 1 (does not count as a stitch), 2sc (UK dc), *ch 1, miss 1 st, 1sc (UK dc); repeat from * to end, join with a sl st to 1st sth, change col at end of rnd.

Rnd 3: Ch 1 (does not count as a stitch), *1sc (UK dc), ch 1, miss 1 st; repeat from * to end, join with a sl st to 1st st.

Repeat Rnds 2 and 3 in the given col sequence, finishing with Rnd 2 in Charcoal Heather. Do not fasten off.

Turn after the last round.

Next rnd (wrong side): Using hook K (7mm), sc (UK dc) into each sc (UK dc) and ch.

Top edge: Using hook K (7mm) and Charcoal Heather with wrong side facing, work sc (UK dc) into each starting ch, either side of the hood.

Finishing off

Hood edge: Using Hook K (7mm) and Charcoal Heather, work *1sc (UK dc), ch 1; repeat from * to end.

Make a pompom of 7cm (2³/₄in) diameter in Midnight Marl (see "How it's done") and sew to the hood. Sew in all yarn ends.

Soft Waves

Flowing movements

Level of difficulty 3

DIMENSIONS

Circumference 146cm (57½in)

Height 28cm (11in)

MATERIALS

Schachenmayr original Merino Extrafine 120 (131yd/1¾oz, 120m/50g) in Cream (Col 102) and Anemone

(Col 148), 3½oz (100g) each, and Plum (Col 146), Eggplant (Col 149), Violet (Col b 147) and Wisteria (Col 145), 1¾oz (50g) each

Hook size H (5mm)

TENSION

In the wavy pattern

with hook size H (5mm)

18 sts and 16 rows = 10 x 10cm (4 x 4in)

PATTERN

Page 91

Colour sequence

*2 rnds in Anemone, 2 rnds in Cream, 2 rnds in Plum, 2 rnds in Cream, 2 rnds in Eggplant, 2 rnds in cream, 2 rnds in Violet, 2 rnds in Cream, 2 rnds in Wisteria, 2 rnds in Cream, rep from * once then work 2 rnds in Anemone.

Instructions

See Chart. Work in the col sequence given.

Using Hook H (5mm) and Anemone, ch 234, join in a ring with a sl st.

Rnd 1: Ch 3 (counts as a stitch), 1dc (UK tr) in 5th ch from hook, 1dc (UK tr), 3hdc (UK htr), 6sc (UK dc), 3hdc (UK htr), 3dc (UK tr), *3dc (UK tr), 3hdc (UK htr), 6sc (UK dc), 3hdc (UK htr), 3dc (UK tr); repeat from * to end, sl st into 3rd starting ch (234 sts).

Rnd 2: Ch 3 (counts as a stitch), 2dc (UK tr), 3hdc (UK htr), 6sc (UK dc), 3hdc (UK htr), 3dc (UK tr), *3dc (UK tr), 3hdc (UK htr), 6sc (UK dc), 3hdc (UK htr), 3dc (UK tr); repeat from * to end, sl st into 3rd starting ch, change col at end of rnd.

Rnd 3: Ch 1 (counts as a stitch), sc (UK dc) in each st to end, sl st into 1st st.

Rnd 4: Work as Rnd 3, change col at end of rnd.

Rnd 5: Ch 1 (counts as a stitch), 2sc (UK dc), 3hdc (UK htr), 6dc (UK tr), 3hdc (UK htr), 3sc (UK dc), *3sc (UK dc), 3hdc (UK htr), 6dc (UK tr), 3hdc (UK htr), 3sc (UK dc); repeat from * to end, sl st into 1st st.

Rnd 6: Work as Rnd 5, changing col at end of rnd.

Rnd 7 and 8: Work as Rnd 3, changing col at end of Rnd 8.

Repeat Rnds 1 to 8 another 4 times, then Rnds 1 to 2 once in Anemone.

Next rnd: With Anemone, ch 1 (counts as a stitch), sc (UK dc) in each st to end. Fasten off.

Finishing off

Fold the loop in half with the right sides facing and sew up approx. 21cm (8¼in) for the hood. Sew in all yarn ends.

Soft Waves

Wild Berries

Wild Berries

Long fringes

Level of difficulty 2

DIMENSIONS

Hood

Width 41cm (16in) Height 30cm (11³/₄in)

Scarf ends

Length with fringes 86cm (33³/₄in)

Width 16cm (6¹/₄in)

MATERIALS

Schachenmayr original Merino Super Big Mix (87½yd/3½oz, 80m/100g) in Black (Col 99), 10³/₅oz (300g), in Burgundy (Col 32) and Fuchsia (Col 36), 7oz (200g) each

Hook size L (8mm)

TENSION

In pattern

with hook size L (8mm)

11dc (UK tr) and 5 rows = 10 × 10cm (4 × 4in)

PATTERN

Page 92

Colour sequence

*Work 1 row each in Black, Burgundy, Black and Fuchsia, repeat from *.

Instructions

See Chart. All rows are worked on the right side.

Using Hook L (8mm) and Black, ch 142 loosely.

Row 1: Ch 3 (counts as a stitch), dc (UK tr) in 5th ch from hook, dc (UK tr) in each ch to end (142 sts). Fasten off.

Row 2: Join relevant col in first st on right side, ch 3 (counts as a stitch), *miss 1 st, 1dc (UK tr), 1dc (UK tr) into the missed st, 1dc (UK tr) into the next st (after the crossed dc [UK tr]); repeat from * to end. Fasten off.

Row 3: Join Black in first st on right side, ch 3 (counts as a stitch), dc (UK tr) in each st to end. Fasten off.

Rows 4 to 9: Repeat Rows 2 to 3 another 3 times in relevant colours.

Mark the middle of the scarf after row 9. With right side facing, count 23 sts to the right of the middle. Starting at this point work the middle 46 sts in the pattern, for a further 14 rows continuing the col sequence.

Finishing off

Fold the hood in half with the right sides facing and sew up in Black yarn.

Using hook L (8mm) and Black work 1 row in sc (UK dc) around the front edge of the hood, working 2sc (UK dc) into each row end. Attach fringes of the desired length to the scarf (see "How it's done").

Ice Age

Hood in a square

Level of difficulty 3

DIMENSIONS

Hood

Width 25cm (9³/₄in)

Height 25cm (9³/₄in)

Scarf ends

Length right 30cm (11³/₄in), left 67cm (26¹/₂in)

Width 15cm (6in)

MATERIALS

Schachenmayr original Merino Super Big Mix (87¹/₂/3¹/₂oz, 80m/100g) in Turquoise (Col 69), 7oz (200g), and in Ocean Color (Col 188), 14oz (400g)

Hook size L (8mm)

TENSION

In the square pattern

with hook size L (8mm)

8 sts and 6 rows = 8 × 8cm (3¹/₄ × 3¹/₄in)

In the scarf pattern

with hook size L (8mm)

10 sts and 8 rows = 10 × 9cm (4 × 3¹/₂in)

PATTERN AND DIAGRAM

Page 94

Square pattern

Work Chart A in rows. The arrow indicates the start ch, the numbers at the two sides mark the beginning of each row.

Scarf pattern

Work Chart B in rows. The chart gives the full width of the scarf. The numbers on both sides indicate the beg of the row. Work rows 1 and 2 once, then repeat rows 3 and 4. Work the dc (UK tr) rfp around the dc (UK tr) 2 rows below (called dc [UK tr] rfp 2 below in the instructions).

Instructions

Hood

Side pieces (make 2)

See Chart A.

Using hook L (8mm) and Turquoise, ch 2.

Row 1: Work 3sc (UK dc) into the 1st ch, turn (3 sts).

Row 2: Ch 1 (does not count as a stitch), 1sc (UK dc), 3sc (UK dc) into next st, 1sc (UK dc), turn (5 sts).

Row 3: Ch 2 (counts as a stitch), dc (UK tr) 2tog in the base of the 2 ch just worked and the next st, 5dc (UK tr) in next st, 1dc (UK tr), dc (UK tr) 2tog in same st as just worked and the last st, turn (9 sts).

Row 4: Ch 1 (does not count as a stitch), 1sc (UK dc) in each st to the corner st, 3sc (UK dc) into corner st, sc (UK dc) in each st to end, turn (11 sts).

Row 5: Ch 2 (counts as a stitch), dc (UK tr) 2tog in the base of the 2 ch just worked and the next st, 1dc (UK tr) in each st to the corner st, 5dc (UK tr) in corner st, 1dc (UK tr) in each st to the last st, dc (UK tr) 2tog in same st as just worked and the last st, turn (15 sts).

Rows 6 to 13: Repeat Rows 4 to 5 another 4 times (39 sts).

Row 14: Ch 1 (does not count as a stitch), 1sc (UK dc) in each st to the end. Fasten off.

Ice Age

Outer strip

Using hook L (8mm) and Turquoise, ch 39. This will be the middle of the final outer strip.

Row 1 (wrong side): Ch 1 (counts as a stitch), 1sc (UK dc) in 2nd ch from hook, 1sc (UK dc) in each ch to end, turn (39 sts).

Row 2: Ch 2 (counts as a stitch), dc (UK tr) 2tog in the base of the 2 ch just worked and the next st, 1dc (UK tr) in each st to the last st, dc (UK tr) 2tog in same st as just worked and the last st, turn.

Row 3: Ch 1 (does not count as a stitch), 1sc (UK dc) in each st to end, turn.

Row 4: Work as Row 2. Fasten off.

With wrong side of completed strip facing, and the starting ch at the top, join Turquoise to the first ch.

Row 1: Ch 1 (counts as a stitch), work 1sc (UK dc) into each ch to the end, turn (39 sts).

Complete as for first half of strip from Row 2 to 4.

Join the side pieces to the middle strip as shown in the schematic. The diagram shows the left side piece and middle strip, and the broken line represents the increases along the diagonal. Place the left side piece on the middle strip with the wrong sides facing and the stitch loops lined up. Slip st the two pieces together with Ocean Color, stitch by stitch, inserting the hook through from the side piece. Slip st the right side piece of the hood onto the other side of the strip. Again, insert the hook from the side piece. Front hood edge: With right side facing, join Ocean Color to the first st at the bottom of the right side of the hood, ch 1 (does not count as a stitch), 1sc (UK dc) in corner of hood, *ch 1, 1sc (UK dc); repeat from * evenly around the hood to the other corner.

Bottom hood edge: With right side facing, join Turquoise to the first st at the bottom of the left side of the hood, ch 1 (does not count as a stitch), work 22sc (UK dc) to middle back of hood, work 22 sc (UK dc) from middle back of hood to right side of the hood.

These 44 sts will be joined to the scarf later on.

Scarf

See Chart B.

Using hook L (8mm) and Ocean Color, ch 13.

Row 1: Ch 3 (counts as a stitch), 1dc (UK tr) in 4th ch from hook, 1dc (UK tr) in each ch to end, turn (14 sts).

Row 2: Ch 1 (does not count as a stitch), 1sc (UK dc) in each st to end, turn.

Row 3: Ch 3 (counts as a stitch), 1dc (UK tr) in next st, (1dc [UK tr] rfp 2 below, 2dc [UK tr]) 4 times, turn.

Row 4: Ch 1 (does not count as a stitch), 1sc (UK dc) in each st to end, turn.

Repeat Rows 3 and 4 until work measures approx 143cm (56$^{1}/_{4}$in), ending with a Row 3.

Do not cut the yarn, crochet around the scarf by working 2sc (UK dc) into the same stitch at the corners, work 1 ch, 1sc (UK dc) down the long side, working the sc (dc) around the edge dc (UK tr) or edge ch, and work 1sc (UK dc) into each st on the short sides.

Finishing off

Lay the scarf down horizontally. Measure approx 30cm (11$^{3}/_{4}$in) from the right edge and mark. Count 44 stitches from this mark, and make another mark.

Place the marked scarf sts at the edges of the hood, and sew the two pieces together in Ocean Color.

NOTE

The short end of the scarf will be on the front when you wear it, and the longer one down the back. If you want to wind the longer scarf end around your neck, just continue crocheting until it is the length you desire.

Mexican Theme

It's got to have tassels

Scarf pattern

Work Chart A in rows. The numbers on both sides indicate the beg of the row. Work rows 1 to 3 once, then repeat rows 4 to 9 increasing 1 st at each end of row 7 as shown. Work rows 4 and 5, (marked in grey in the pattern) in turn in *Pink, Apple Green, Royal, repeat from *. Work all other rows in Suede. When changing colours, finish the last st in the row in the next col.

Hood pattern

Work Chart C in rows. The numbers on the sides indicate the beginning of the row. Repeat rows 1 to 10. The sc (UK dc) of the previous row are shown below the first row. Work rows 1, 3 and 7, (marked grey in the pattern) on the right side in turn in *Royal, Pink, Apple Green, Pink, repeat from *. Work all other rows in Suede.

Level of difficulty 2

DIMENSIONS

Hood

Width 25cm (9³/₄in)

Height 30cm (11³/₄in)

Scarf ends

Length 49cm (19¼in)

Width 21cm (8¼in)

MATERIALS

Schachenmayr original Merino Extrafine 85 (93yd/1¾oz, 85m/50g) in Suede (Col 212), 8⁴/₅oz (250g), Pink (Col 237), Apple Green (Col 273) and Royal (Col 251), 1¾oz (50g) each

Hook size J (6mm)

TENSION

In the scarf pattern

with hook size J (6mm)

15 sts and 6 rows = 10 × 6cm (4 × 2¹/₂in)

In the hood pattern

with hook size J (6mm)

15 sts and 12 rows = 10 × 12.5cm (4 × 5in)

PATTERN

Instructions

Scarf

See Chart A. Work in given col sequence.

Using Hook J (6mm) and Suede, ch 8.

Row 1: Ch 3 (counts as a stitch), 2dc (UK tr) in 4th ch from hook, (1dc [UK tr], 2dc [UK tr] in next st) 3 times, 1dc (UK tr) in last st, turn (13 sts).

Row 2: Ch 3 (counts as a stitch), (2dc [UK tr], 2dc[UK tr] in next st, 3dc [UK tr]) twice, turn (15 sts).

Row 3: Ch 1 (does not count as a stitch), (1sc [UK dc], ch 1, miss 1 st) 7 times, 1sc (UK dc) in last st, change col at end of row, turn.

Row 4: Ch 1 (does not count as a stitch), 1sc (UK dc), *1sc (UK dc), ch 1, miss 1 st; rep from * to last 2 sts, 2sc (UK dc), turn.

Row 5: Ch 1 (does not count as a stitch), *1sc (UK dc), ch 1, miss 1 st; repeat from * to last st, 1sc (UK dc) in last st, change col at end of row, turn.

Row 6: Ch 1 (does not count as a stitch), 1sc (UK dc), *1sc (UK dc), ch 1, miss 1 st; rep from * to last 2 sts, 2sc (UK dc), turn.

Row 7: Ch 3 (counts as a stitch), 1dc (UK tr) in same st, 1dc (UK tr) in each st to the last 2 sts, 2dc (UK tr) in next st, 1dc (UK tr), turn (17 sts).

Row 8: Ch 3 (counts as a stitch), 1dc (UK tr) in each st to end, turn.

Mexican Theme

Row 9: Ch 1 (does not count as a stitch), *1sc (UK dc), ch 1, miss 1 st; repeat from * to last st, 1sc (UK dc) in last st, change col at end of row, turn.

Repeat rows 4 to 9 in col sequence given another 6 times, then rows 4 to 7 once (31 sts).

Work should measure approx 49cm (19¼in).

Cut yarn and set work aside.

Work the right side of the scarf in the same way. Join the two together in Row 50 as shown in Chart B. The chart only shows the outer sts of the two parts (1 = left piece, 2 = right piece). The yarn end of the left piece of the scarf is marked by a *. Row 50: Work as Row 8 to the end of the right piece of the scarf, ch 11 after the last dc (UK tr), then continue working as Row 8 over the left piece of the scarf (73 sts).

Row 51: Ch 1 (does not count as a stitch), 1sc (UK dc) in each stitch and ch to end, turn.

Row 52: Ch 1 (does not count as a stitch), 1sc (UK dc) in each stitch to end, turn.

Row 53: Work as Row 52, changing col at end of row for start of hood pattern.

Continue in the hood pattern. See Chart C. Work in given col sequence.

Row 1: Ch 2 (counts as a stitch), 1dc (UK tr) in same st, *miss 2 sts, 3dc (UK tr) in next st; repeat from * to last 3 sts, miss 2 sts, 2dc (UK tr) in last st. Fasten off.

Row 2: With right side facing, join Suede to first st, ch 2 (counts as a stitch), 1dc (UK tr) in same st, *miss 2 sts, (1dc [UK tr], ch 1, 1dc [UK tr]) in next st; repeat from * to last 3 sts, miss 2 sts, 2dc (UK tr) in last st. Fasten off.

Row 3: With right side facing, join relevant col to first st, ch 2 (counts as a stitch), 1dc (UK tr) in same st, *miss 2 sts, (1dc [UK tr], ch 1, 1dc [UK tr]) in next st; repeat from * to last 3 sts, miss 2 sts, 2dc (UK tr) in last st. Fasten off.

Row 4: With right side facing, join Suede to first st, ch 2 (counts as a stitch), 1dc (UK tr) in each st and ch to end, turn.

Row 5: Ch 3 (counts as a stitch), 1dc (UK tr) in each st to end, turn.

Row 6: Ch 1 (does not count as a stitch), 1sc (UK dc) in each st to end. Fasten off.

Row 7: With right side facing, join relevant col to first st, ch 2 (counts as a stitch), *ch 1, miss 1 st, cluster in next st; rep from * to last 2 sts, ch 1, miss 1st, 1dc (UK tr) in last st. Fasten off.

Rows 8 to 10: Work as Rows 4 to 6.

Repeat Rows 1 to 10 once, then Row 1 once working in given col sequence, ending with Apple Green.

Next row: With right side facing, join Suede to first st, ch 2 (counts as a stitch), 1dc (UK tr) in each st to end. Fasten off.

Hood height should be approx. 30cm(11¾in). Cut the yarn, leaving it fairly long.

Finishing off

Fold hood in half with the right sides together and, with the long end, sew up the top seam of the hood using whipstitch. Include the stitch loops of the opposite layers with each stitch.

Work 1 row of crab stitch (see "How it's done") in Suede around the scarf pieces and hood, starting at the beginning of the scarf ends. Tighten the ends of the scarves by threading the yarn through the first row of sts, and secure the ends well.

Make 3 tassels in Suede with Pink ties (see "How it's done"). Sew the tassels onto the ends of the scarves and the tip of the hood.

Fold the tip of the hat downwards slightly to form a triangle. Sew the tip in Suede, working between the two last rows of dc (UK tr) on the underside. Sew in all yarn ends.

How it's done

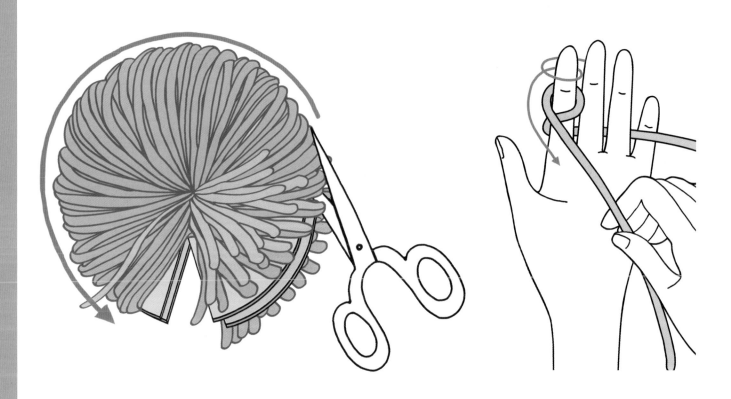

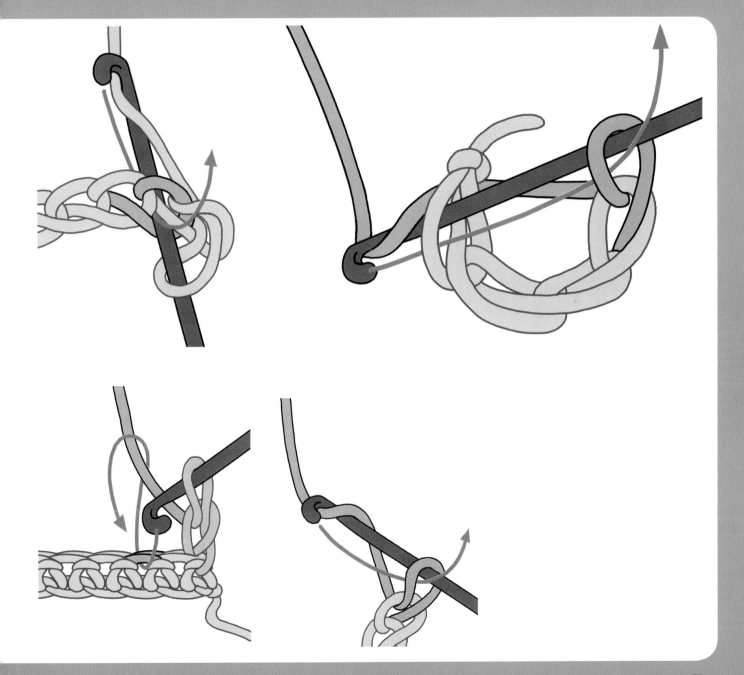

CHAIN STITCHES (CASTING ON)

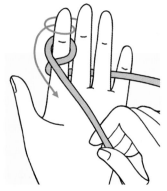

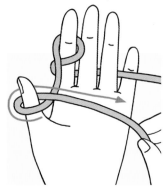

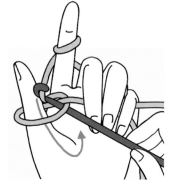

Before you start crocheting, make a loop.

1 Hold the yarn between your little and ring fingers, and thread it behind your middle finger.
Now wind the yarn around your index finger and thumb. The end of the yarn will be in your hand.

2 Now pick up the hook and draw the yarn from your index finger through the loop around your thumb. Then take your thumb out of the loop.

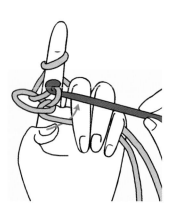

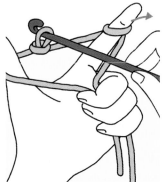

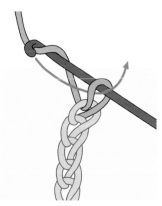

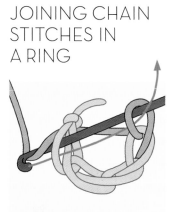

JOINING CHAIN STITCHES IN A RING

3 Push your thumb under the end of the yarn that you are holding in your middle, ring and little fingers.

4 Then spread your thumb and index finger, and tighten the starting loop on the hook. You should be able to move it on the hook, but it must not slide off.

5 In order to cast on more chains, use the hook to draw the yarn through the loop on your index finger and through the loop on your finger. This creates a chain, also known as chain stitch or ch.

To join a row of chain stitches in a ring, insert the hook in the first chain, draw the yarn through and pull it through the chain and the loop on the hook.

STITCH LOOPS

Each crocheted stitch creates a loop with yarn at the front and behind it. The instructions contain three different ways of inserting the hook in the stitches, all of which create different effects.
1 Through both of the loops of the stitch
2 Through the front loop of the stitch
3 Through the back loop of the stitch

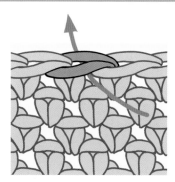 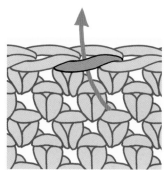 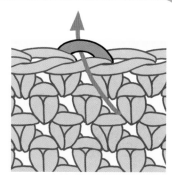

1 As a general rule, unless the instructions say otherwise, work through both loops of the stitch.

2 If you work through the front loop only, you can create textured stitches such as bobbles or frills.

3 If you work through the back loop only, it creates a little ridge (made by the front loops of the stitches) that not only looks attractive but can also help when sewing together.

SLIP STITCHES

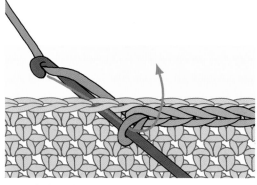

Insert the hook in the next stitch and place the yarn around the hook. Draw the yarn through both of the loops on the hook.

CRAB STITCH

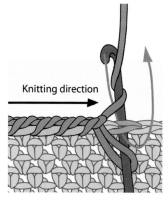 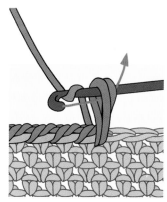

Knitting direction

1 Insert the hook from front to back through the sc (UK dc) in the previous row on the right. The loop on the hook will be flat against the crocheting. Now draw the yarn through...

2 ...and pull both loops upwards so the stitch isn't too tight. The loops will be close together on the hook. Draw the yarn through both loops.

SINGLE CROCHET (UK DOUBLE CROCHET)

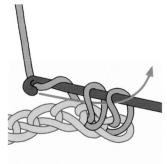

1 Insert the hook in the second chain from the hook and draw the yarn through by hooking it from the back to the front and drawing it through the chain stitch. You will now have 2 loops on the hook.

2 Now yarn over hook and draw the yarn (from the back to the front) through both loops.

3 Insert the hook in the next stitch and repeat.

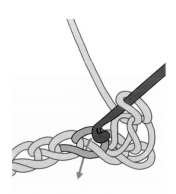
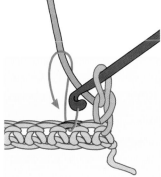

4 If you are crocheting rows of sc (UK dc), turn the work at the end of each row. Before you start working sc (UK dc) again, ch 1 as a starting chain. Then insert the hook in the next stitch of the previous row and crochet more sc (UK dc).

DOUBLE CROCHET (UK TREBLE)

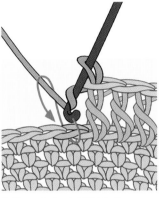 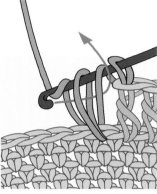 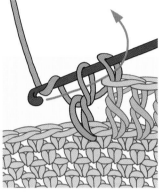

1 To crochet a dc (UK tr), place the yarn around the hook and insert the hook in the next stitch of the previous row. Draw the yarn through the stitch. You will now have 3 loops on the hook.

2 Yarn over hook and draw the yarn through 2 of the 3 loops.

3 You will now have 2 loops on the hook. Yarn over hook again and draw the yarn through the 2 remaining loops.

HALF DOUBLE CROCHET (UK HALF TREBLE)

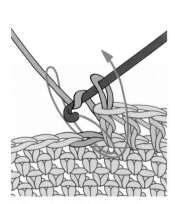 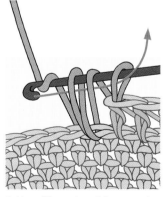 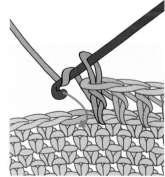

1 To work a half double crochet (hdc) (UK half treble [htr]), place the yarn around the hook, then insert in the next stitch and draw the yarn through.

2 You will now have 3 loops on the hook. Yarn over hook and draw the yarn through all 3 loops.

3 Repeat to make further half double crochet (UK half trebles).

DOUBLE CROCHET (UK TREBLE) ROUND FRONT POST

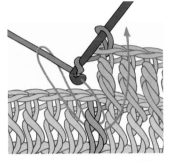 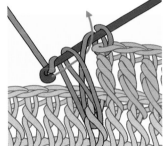

1 To crochet a double crochet (UK treble) round the front post, place the yarn around the hook and insert it from front to back to front around the double crochet (UK treble) in the previous row. Yarn over and draw yarn though.

2 You will have 3 loops on the hook. Yarn over hook hook and draw through 2 of the 3 loops. Yarn over hook and draw yarn through the remaining loops.

DOUBLE CROCHET (UK TREBLE) ROUND BACK POST

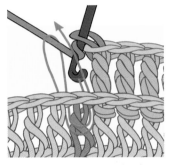 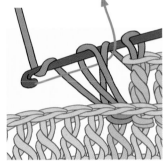

1 To crochet a double crochet (UK treble) round the back post, place the yarn around the hook and insert it from back to front to back around the double crochet (UK treble) in the previous row. Yarn over and draw through.

2 You will have 3 loops on the hook. Yarn over hook and draw through 2 of the 3 loops. Yarn over hook and draw yarn through the remaining loops.

CHANGING COLOURS

If you are working to a stripy pattern and want to change colours, work the first part of the last sc (UK dc) in the previous round in the old colour so you have 2 loops on the hook. Finish these loops in the new colour. The last sc (UK dc) will have been worked in the old colour, but the loop on the hook will now be in the new colour.

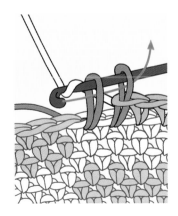

INCREASE STITCHES

If you want to increase individual stitches, then all you do is work a second stitch of the same type into the same place. You can increase any kind of stitch this way, and you can increase in rounds or rows. The number of stitches increases by 1 each time.

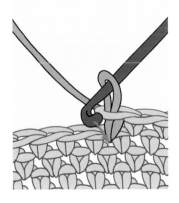

DECREASE STITCHES

Decrease two single crochet (UK double crochet) together

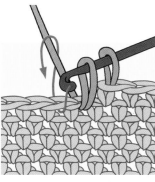

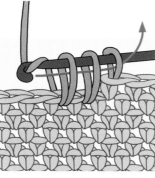

1 If you want to decrease (dec) 2 single (UK double) crochet together, draw 1 loop through and onto the hook in each of the 2 stitches.

2 Then place the yarn over the hook again and draw it through all of the loops on the hook. This reduces the number of stitches by 1.

Decreasing double crochet (UK treble)

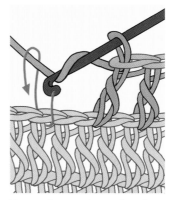

You can decrease the number of double crochet (UK treble) simply by leaving them out. Instead of working a double crochet (UK treble) into each stitch, simply miss one.

Decrease two double crochet (UK trebles) together

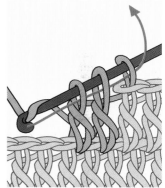

Work half of the first double crochet (UK treble) in the first stitch. You will have 2 loops on the hook. Then work half of another double crochet (UK treble) in the second stitch. You will have 3 loops on the hook. Now place the yarn over the hook and draw through all 3 loops. This reduces the number of stitches by 1.

FINISHING OFF

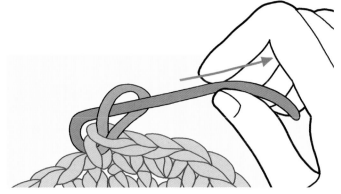

1 Once you have finished your work, cut the yarn leaving a length of approx. 10cm (4in) after the last stitch. Wrap the yarn around the hook and draw it all the way through the last stitch.

2 Pull the end of the yarn – and you have a firm knot.

SEWING UP

Backstitch

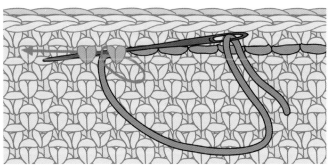

Backstitch is worked close to the outer edge. Place the crocheted pieces together neatly, and if necessary secure them with pins. Now insert the needle through the back of the work to the front, and insert it from the front of the work to the back again. Repeat.

Whipstitch

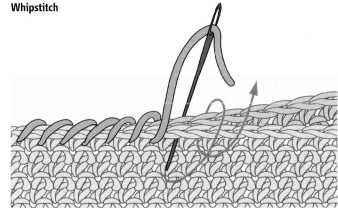

Place the crocheted pieces together neatly. Now insert the needle through both items from the back through to the front, then from the front to the back through the next stitch. Repeat.

POMPOMS

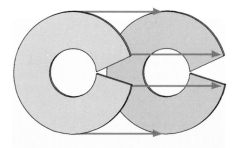

1 Cut out two cardboard discs of the diameter of the required pompom, and cut a V into the side of each to make an opening. Place the two discs together.

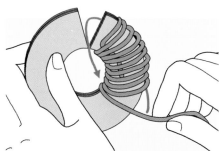

2 Now wind the yarn around both discs until you have filled the hole in the middle. It's easy to guide the needle through the opening cut made earlier.

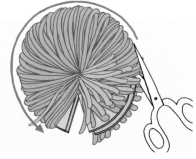

3 Cut around the edges of the yarn between the cardboard discs.

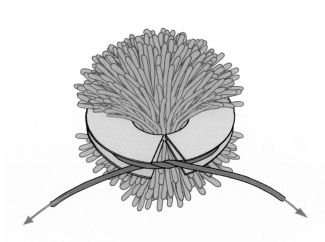

4 Take a piece of yarn, place it in the middle of the cardboard discs and knot it tightly.

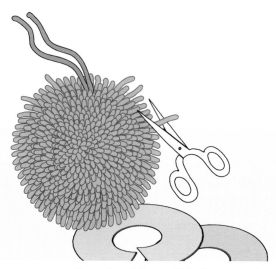

5 You can now remove the cardboard discs, and trim the pompom into a nice round shape.

TASSELS

FRINGES

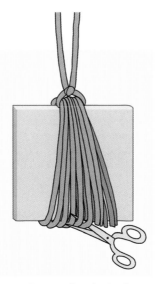

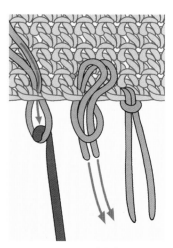

1 Cut a rectangle out of cardboard. Make it roughly as wide as you want the tassel to be long. Wrap yarn evenly around the cardboard. The more you wind, the thicker the tassel will be.

2 Cut the yarn. Thread a darning needle with a fairly long piece of yarn. Feed it under the yarns along the edge of the cardboard, and secure it with a knot. Now you can cut through the bundle of yarn at the bottom.

3 Bind the bundle at the top. Use another long thread for this. Shape one end into a loop and hold it on the yarn bundle. Wind the remainder of the yarn firmly around the bundle. The end of the loop should peep out at the top, the loop at the bottom. Make a few winds, then feed the yarn through the loop, take hold of both ends and pull. Trim any straggly ends.

Cut a rectangle 2cm (¾in) longer than the desired fringes out of cardboard. Wrap yarn evenly and not too tightly around the cardboard. Cut open the threads add the bottom, and carefully remove the doubled threads from the cardboard. Insert a suitable crochet hook in the end of the crocheted items. Hook it around the middle of the doubled thread, and draw through the item to make a loop. Draw the ends of the thread through this loop, and carefully tighten. When you have finished, trim all the fringes to the same length.

Symbols

o = 1 chain (ch)

● = 1 slip stitch (sl st)

✕ = 1 single crochet (sc) (UK double crochet [dc])

⩟ = 1 sc (UK dc) into back horizontal stitch loop (BLO) in previous row or round

↓ = 3 sc (UK dc) into same stitch

⋏ = decrease sc (UK dc) 2tog: draw yarn through each of 2 neighbouring stitches, yarn around hook and draw through all 3 loops

⟁ = decrease sc (UK dc) 2tog: draw yarn through each of 3 neighbouring stitches, yarn around hook and draw through all 4 loops

T = 1 half double crochet (hdc) (UK half treble [htr])

⋀ = decrease hdc (UK htr) 2tog: (yoh and insert hook into appropriate stitch and draw loop through) twice. Yoh and draw through all 5 loops

 = bobble made from 3 half double crochet (UK half treble) decreased together: (yoh, insert hook in 1 stitch and draw loop through) 3 times. Yoh and draw through all 7 loops

⊤ = 1 double crochet (dc) (UK treble [tr])

 = crossed dc (UK tr)

 = (dc (UK tr), ch 1, dc [UK tr]) into same stitch

 = 2dc (UK tr) into same stitch

 = decrease: dc (UK tr) 2tog

 = 3 dc (UK tr) into same stitch

 = decrease: dc (UK tr) 3tog

 = cluster: 3 dc (UK tr) together in same stitch

 = dc (UK tr) rfp (round front post):

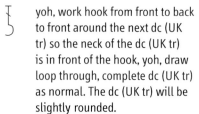 yoh, work hook from front to back to front around the next dc (UK tr) so the neck of the dc (UK tr) is in front of the hook, yoh, draw loop through, complete dc (UK tr) as normal. The dc (UK tr) will be slightly rounded.

= dc (UK tr) rbp (round back post): yoh, work hook from back to front to back around the next dc (UK tr) so the neck of the dc (UK tr) is behind the hook, yoh, draw loop through, complete dc (UK tr) as normal. The dc (UK tr) will be slightly rounded.

NOTE

If symbols are joined at the bottom, this means the stitches are worked into the same stitch.

If the symbols are joined at the top, it means they are decreased together. Work each stitch as far as the last loop, then yoh and draw through all the remaining loops together.

Evergreen

Page 12

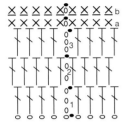

Soft Waves

Page 64

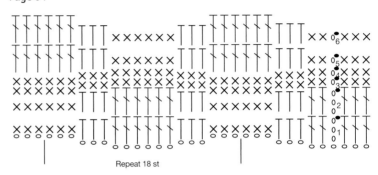

Repeat 18 st

Lady in Red

Page 42

Pattern A

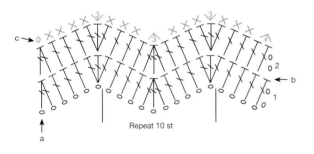

Repeat 10 st

Pattern B

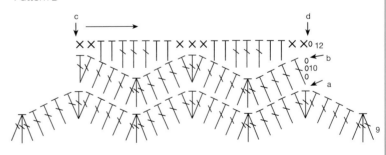

Diagram

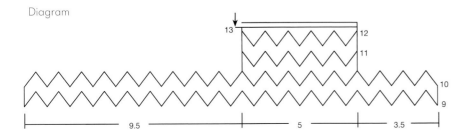

Multicolour

Page 28

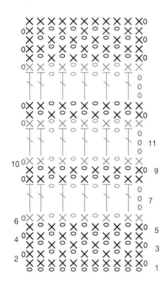

Wild Berries

Page 67

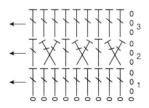

Orange

Page 8

Pattern A

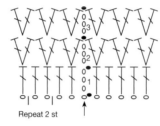

Repeat 2 st

Pattern B

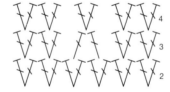

Warm Up

Page 46

Pattern A

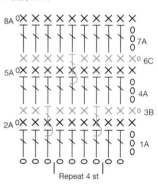

Repeat 4 st

Pattern B

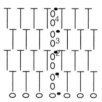

Hot Red

Page 15

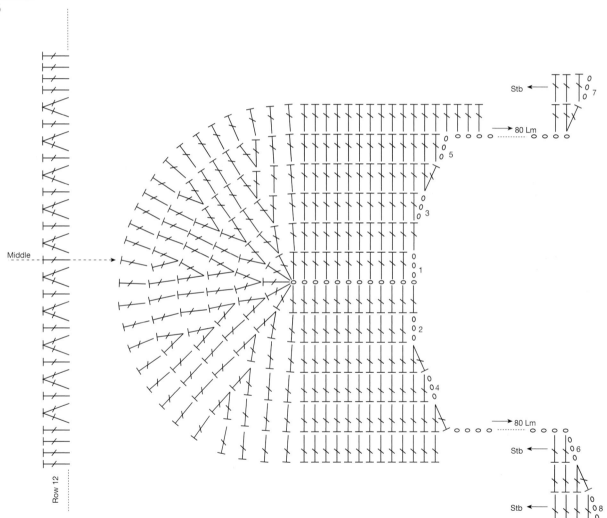

Middle

Row 12

Stb

80 Lm

5

3

1

2

4

7

80 Lm

Stb

6

Stb

8

Mexican Theme

Page 74

Pattern A

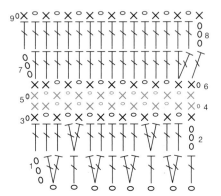

Pattern C

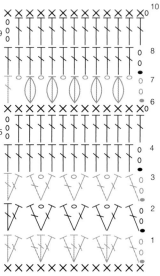

Pattern B

Scarf piece ①   Scarf piece ②

Ice Age

Page 70

Pattern A

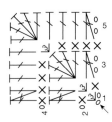

Pattern B

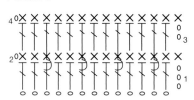

Diagram

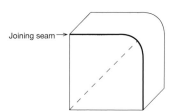

Joining seam →

Rockabilly

Page 36

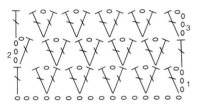

Coral Reef

Page 50

Pattern A

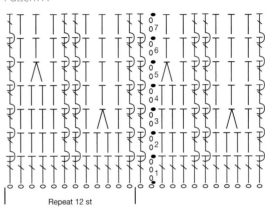

Repeat 12 st

Pattern B

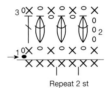

Repeat 2 st

Blue Velvet

Page 18

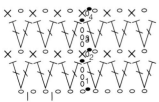

Repeat 2 st

Grey Shadow

Page 60

Pattern A

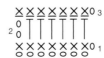

Pattern B

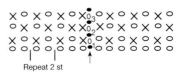

Repeat 2 st

First published in Great Britain 2016
Search Press Limited
Wellwood, North Farm Road,
Tunbridge Wells, Kent TN2 3DR

Original German title published as *So Scoodie*

Text copyright © 2014 frechverlag GmbH, 70499 Stuttgart

English Translation by Burravoe Translation Services

Typesetting by Greengate Publishing Services, Tonbridge

Photographs: frechverlag GmbH, 70499 Stuttgart; lichtpunkt, Michael Ruder, Stuttgart

ISBN: 978-1-78221-302-4

Suppliers:
If you have difficulty in obtaining any of the materials and equipment mentioned in this book, then please visit the Search Press website for details of suppliers: www.searchpress.com

Printed in China

Acknowledgements
Our thanks to Coats (www.coats-gmbh.de) for supporting us with the materials and to ID-Bike GmbH – Elmoto for the loan of a light electric motorcycle (www.elmoto.com).